Praise for Monica Packer and *Sticky Habits*

"*Sticky Habits* is a refreshing, compassionate guide to building habits that last. Monica's realistic approach ditches perfectionism and helps women create supportive habits that actually fit their full lives."

—Jess Massey, *founder of Hustle Sanely*

"Practical. Realistic. Fun. Finally, a habit-building road map designed by and for women."

—Taylor Morrison, *author of Inner Workout*

"Monica lays out a clear road map for even the busiest women to build habits that are personal, practical, and possible. Drawing on years of meaningful experience, *Sticky Habits* offers a compassionate and empowering approach."

—Miranda Anderson, MAPP, BSN, RN,
host of the Practically Happy podcast

Sticky Habits

Sticky Habits

A Woman's Guide to Reclaim Happiness, Ditch Perfectionism, and Create Habits that Last

Monica Packer

JOSSEY-BASS™
A Wiley Brand

Published by John Wiley & Sons, Inc., Hoboken, New Jersey.

Library of Congress Control Number: 2026017305

ISBN: 9781394401161 (Hardback)
ISBN: 9781394401178 (ePub)
ISBN: 9781394401185 (ePDF)

Cover Design: Jon Boylan
Cover Image: © eyewave/stock.adobe.com
Author Photo: © Hey Becca Photo

SKY10160257_063026

For Brad and our children, who both inspired and supported changes in me that led to this work

Disclaimer

This book is for women.

Even the words *women*, *woman*, and *female* aren't simple descriptors of the select demographic I seek to reach. I acknowledge that much of what I share in this book may feel best applied to those in hetero-normative bodies and/or relationships. Thanks to the research most readily available as well as the majority of women I have served online for 10 years, that is indeed the case. If you don't subscribe to the gendered models I teach, I hope you will still find a great deal of helpful information in this book. None of what I share is meant to be ignorant of your life experiences, and I hope you'll still feel welcome to learn.

All personal anecdotes I share in this book are my own and recounted to the best of my ability. Other stories also shared were done with permission. Names, personal details, and story specifics may have been changed to protect privacy.

Contents

Preface: What Reclaiming Happiness Has to Do with Sticky Habits

Learn: How habits go deeper to women feeling like themselves, and why this matters

When I think of "happy," I think of my mom and her naturally sunny personality. Throughout my life, she's told me, "Even when I'm sad, I wake up happy." That gene must have skipped me; I tend to feel more burdened than cheerful.

It's mystifying to me that the descriptive word under my ninth-grade photo was *optimistic.* As an adult, I have found myself veering more toward *cynical.* Perhaps my original sunny gene gradually wore off with time. Maybe age and life experiences incrementally shifted my inclination from happy to grumpy.

I've dealt with clinical depression a few times in my life, the kind that scares you and the people who love you. The first particularly bad bout happened when I was a college student held captive by a perfectionism that led to multiple eating disorders, and with them panic attacks, anxiety, and suicidal ideation. This depression returned about eight years later as an underachieving perfectionist while I was a young mother of two (and later three) little ones. Despite being in the prime "Those were the days" times, I felt anything but fulfilled.

While I thankfully recovered from these episodes, I still ride the mental health rollercoaster that occasionally dips into anxiety, stress, and sadness.

And yet, I would describe myself as "happy." Why, when I'm admittedly not an optimist? Why, when I regularly feel overwhelmed by my daily duties? Why, when I occasionally struggle with confidence?

It's actually quite simple: **I feel like myself.**

So, I guess I've come full circle back to my mother—because, even when I'm sad (read also stressed, angry, overwhelmed, anxious), I still feel like "Monica." And that, to me, *is* happiness.

The Easiest Thing in the World

Feeling like yourself is not easy, especially when that self gets lost to good intentions, namely, trying to be "responsible" and take care of everything (and everyone) on your list. In my 10 years working with women, I have witnessed how it's the easiest thing in the world for us as women to lose ourselves.

It's not only common to slip into a loss of self—it's expected. For women, "good" is often synonymous with "sacrifice." This is especially true for those in caretaking roles—mothers, teachers, nurses, elder care, and so on. It's not just that these roles require the sacrifice of our wants, our time, our bodies, it's that they can easily morph into the sacrifice of our very selves.

I am grateful to be a mother of five children. It's the most important role I carry, one I always wanted. And yet, learning to be a "good" mom followed a different path than the one I originally set out on. The first few years of motherhood, I followed the sacrificial template embedded in my subconscious, I imagine much like how roots suck water from their surrounding soil. I set aside my own ambitions, ignored my needs, and tossed aside my wants, all in the pursuit of being a good mom.

Until it became obvious that these "sacrifices" decidedly made me *not* a good mother.

My story will follow more in the next chapter, but I experienced a pattern I've found so often replicated that it's taken on a sort of archetypal heroine's journey:

- Woman intends to be "good."
- Woman ties goodness with perfectionistic self-sacrifice.
- Woman gives all of her time, energy, and body to others.
- Woman grows tired, angry, sad, and resentful.
- Woman has a choice to make: continue to sacrifice as is or do things differently.

I chose to do things differently.

Little by little, I sought to reclaim my life, make it look and feel more like my own, and grow outside the sacrificial, perfection-driven models that only created unhappiness for me and those I love. I chose to believe that progress mattered more than perfection.

Rediscovering myself not only improved my happiness levels but also helped me have a *self* to give from. And much to my surprise, what made this all possible was having habits that supported that self—the kind of habits that stick.

Sticky Habits

When women are under-supported (both by themselves and by others), habits are too easily grouped under their already long litany of responsibilities: habits of the home, work, body, and relationships. While these are all important priorities in life, life has to be about more than being responsible.

Consistent habits certainly make happiness more possible in women because they make their lives run more smoothly, increase their productivity, or help them achieve what they desire. However, these metrics for successful habits are missing something very important: habits go deeper. Habits are more about the "self" than they are about staying true to a to-do list.

Sticky habits are not only habits that allow you to be consistent but also consistently *you*.

This is something I learned as I sought to form habits for myself—ones where the primary goal was to consistently support my needs, wants, priorities, and happiness, not just my responsibilities. Not only did this pursuit change how I saw habits, it also demanded I do them differently. I found that traditional habit formation methods ignore how women's lives are uniquely laden by responsibilities that very easily derail their habits. Instead, I desired a new way: a method uniquely designed for my life as a busy woman.

A Bigger Purpose

Along my path of progress over perfection, I collected a community of women who were similarly ready for a new way. They wanted to break the patterns set before them, rediscover their identity, and make progress outside of perfectionism. They also wanted their daily lives to both reflect and reinforce their reclaimed selves, something made far more possible through dependable habits. As I shared my habit experiments with them, they joined me. The result? Women who felt like themselves again. In other words, "happy."

In the words of Melinda French Gates, "When we lift up women, we lift up humanity."[1] I am convinced that many of the ills

---

[1] *The Moment of Lift: How Empowering Women Changes the World* (Flatiron Books, 2019).

of this world could be fixed if women had more opportunities to show up as themselves. This work of reclamation—of self, of happiness, of habits—isn't about women being selfish; it's about bolstering their capacity to change the world, a world that already desperately depends on women's selflessness.

This is why I wrote a book on something seemingly both so privileged and menial as habits. Like a healthy trunk spreading its nutrients out to all its branches, when women's lives are better, so are the lives of all those who are connected to them. While grounded in improving each individual woman's life and happiness, the purpose of this work transcends the personal.

What You'll Find in This Book

This book isn't designed to make you more productive; it's designed to help you feel more like yourself.

What you'll find is an alternative to the typical all-or-nothing teachings that most of us have learned since we were kids. You'll learn my Sticky Habit Method, one designed to help women form supportive habits that stick, enabling them to be their "happy" selves even amid their very busy lives. Please trust me now when I tell you that your deep desire to change will be met by a deeper habit method than ones filled with checklists and dependent on "willpower."

Women often call my method "gentle" and "flexible," but it's also transformative. Through my coaching, programs, and podcast, I have guided thousands of women in applying this method and observed its life-changing effects.

The habits I want you to work on are the ones that will help you feel cared for enough to show up as yourself. This will be subjective! For some women, they'll want to start by prioritizing reading or crafting. For others, they'll want to begin with something practical, like meal planning or weightlifting. You get to choose, but I want to urge you now to select habits that will put you on your own priority list, the kind that help you feel like "you."

Sticky Habits is divided into five parts, each of them housing chapters:

- Part One breaks down why women must do habits differently.
- Part Two redefines what habits are and how they are formed.
- Part Three teaches the first half of the Sticky Habit Method.
- Part Four covers the second half of the Sticky Habit Method.
- Part Five teaches how to reform bad habits.

I believe we learn best through stories. I've assigned habit stories throughout this book to help illustrate the concepts inside, but please know—the women featured are real.[2] I not only coached them to learn and apply this method, but I also personally witnessed the mundane-to-maddening challenges they face every day. Some stories will resonate with your own life more than others, but together they illustrate how shifting habits can help us better overcome these obstacles. My own story will also be featured more predominantly in the first chapter, then sprinkled throughout the rest.

There are quite a few terms/concepts/acronyms throughout *Sticky Habits*. To help you keep track, reference the glossary section located at the end of the book. Dog-ear the page to easily flip back to it, as needed.

Finally, at the end of each chapter, you'll see these three categories:

TAKEAWAYS: This is the section where I'll share a brief overview of the most important thoughts/lessons from the chapter. It's a good way to reinforce what you're learning, and something to reference later if you want to be reminded of concepts without rereading.

[2] Some names and personal details have been changed.

TAKE THOUGHT: This is your workbook-style area where you can dig deep *and* get practical with what you're learning. It was important to me that what you learn doesn't just stay in your head but gets down on paper. Feel free to write your reflections directly onto these pages, and do so without fear of writing imperfectly or of others seeing it.

TAKE ACTION: This is where you are given your next steps. In the spirit of progress not perfection, I designed these steps to be doable. You can, of course, do much more, but if I were personally coaching you, I'd consider these steps your baseline ways of applying what you learn.

Before we move on, starting with my own habit story, let's do just one of the three sections as a little warm-up:

TAKE THOUGHT: *How would your life change if you felt more like yourself? What habits would make "happiness" more possible for you?*

NOTE: For more (printables, recommended books, complementary podcast episodes, etc.), remember to check out the free and included Sticky Habit resources, available online at https://stickyhabitsbook.com/resources:

Part One

REBEL: WHY WOMEN DESERVE A HABIT FORMATION METHOD DESIGNED SPECIFICALLY FOR THEM

Chapter 1

A Tale of Two Monicas

***Learn:* My "habit story" and how rediscovering who I am outside perfectionism led to a reclamation of my life, and eventually my habits**

Three kids in, I was a shell of "Monica." On the outside, I could play up the performance of being a capable person, a loving and devoted stay-at-home mother, but on the inside, I was raging. The near-constant simmering anger was the most surprising part of motherhood for me, and I felt awful about it. Most of the time I could keep it at bay, but then I'd find myself blowing up over the smallest of things—from haughtily sweeping up crumbs I didn't make, to literally crying over spilled milk, to having an epic "mommy tantrum" over bubbles. Yes, bubbles.

The kids and I were in the tiny backyard of our old home in Northern California. I sat in a patio chair, patting the back of my infant while monitoring my older two children playing. In an effort to create some fun for them (since I most decidedly wasn't ready for any out-of-the-home adventures), I had given them both a small bottle of bubbles. It was going fine, until my oldest—then barely four years old—accidentally emptied her bubbles all over the two concrete steps leading to our house. I congratulated myself for calmly getting the hose and simply spraying off the slippery solution—no chiding needed.

But then, I heard a scream. And it was coming from inside the house.

I ran in, frantic to locate what must have been a near-death emergency only to find my daughter panicking in her shared bedroom, standing over yet another spilled bottle of bubbles. But, this was no ordinary bottle—this was the giant kind, the kind meant to refill the tiny ones. And it was nearly empty, the solution decidedly soaking not just the wool rug but the old wooden floors underneath it.

I single-handedly went to work on fixing the situation, still clutching my young infant in one hand while I used the other to haul a bucket of water and a pile of towels into the room. All I could think of was money. If the wool rug was ruined, we couldn't afford a new one. If the wood floor underneath the rug got warped, we couldn't pay to repair it.

So, I scrubbed, as quickly and as strongly as I could with my only free hand. But, instead of the solution soaking up into my rags, it lathered and grew. Mini mountains of bubbles began to form and reach higher and higher, wider and wider, until they matched my growing despair. My internal monologue bled into a dramatic performance, one fit for the stage. I found myself wailing, "I'm the ONLY one that can do this—the ONLY ONNNNNNE! It's always on ME!"

As I scrubbed, I screamed. I was barely aware of my children at that moment. The spotlight had zoomed in on this life-or-death plight: me versus bubbles. That is until I happened to look up. There, in the doorway stood my four-year old and my two-year old with frightened faces. When they saw my gaze fall on them, they audibly gasped, then sprinted from the room.

I slumped back on my heels, stunned. I didn't just scare my own children, I scared myself.

This was one of many moments that pushed me to rethink what I thought a "good" mother was. Perhaps the pursuit of self-sacrifice was not just costing me, but also my children, of having a happy home. In my pursuit to embody an impossible ideal, I didn't recognize who I had become.

The "Monica" I used to know was capable, kind, and persistent. She was creative, smart, and ambitious. She was calm, thoughtful, and hard-working. I wasn't the type to throw a tantrum over bubbles. So, why was I? The truth was actually quite simple—it wasn't the crumbs, the milk, or the bubbles; it was that I wasn't taking care of myself.

How could I have been? With my husband, Brad, working long hours with a similarly-long commute into San Francisco, I was essentially the *only* active parent of three very small children, states away from my family, and without a dime to spare to get outside help. I didn't know it yet, but in the coming years two of those children would be diagnosed with multiple special needs. I was hopelessly sleep-deprived—that's a given—but I was also deprived of time *to* and *for* myself. Beyond my exercise regimen, there was no self-care to speak of. And even then, working out looked like pushing a double-wide stroller at breakneck speed, six miles at a time. (This isn't a humble brag! You'll learn in Chapter 6 how I ended up paying a steep price for this practice.)

With so much to be done and only me to do it all, I showed up. I showed up for the kids. For the meals. For the laundry. For the floors. And, heck, even for the toilet. But, I didn't show up for myself. Gone were the self-care moments I used to enjoy, gone were my hobbies of art and creativity, gone were my once-steady habits of journaling, goal making, and reading.

There was simply no time—no time to get lost in a novel, to sew or to copy a creation from Pinterest, to paint my nails with crummy drugstore polish, or to even sit down on the couch and watch an occasional episode of *The Property Brothers*. My choices felt so clear: show up for my responsibilities or show up for myself. Only one or the other. So, I chose my responsibilities over myself.

That was until I saw the frightened faces of my children watching me melt down from their bedroom doorway. It was clear all at once that my self-sacrifice was hurting those things—those people, really—I was sacrificing myself for.

It was this experience that pushed me to find a new way, one that differed from the model of perfection I originally thought I had to follow—not just as a mom, but as a woman. Perhaps there was a way to choose my responsibilities *and* myself?

Thanks to the advice of a new therapist, who immediately targeted my perfectionistic tendencies, I started small. I made a list of 30 things I wanted to try before turning 30.[1] This was not another list of goals to achieve or resolutions to fulfill, but a list of exploration, of self-discovery. I read a novel. I sewed a seat cover for an ugly second-hand settee. I wrote long and now-embarrassing personal essays on a blog that nobody read. I ogled modern art at a museum. I tried a new kind of oatmeal. And I shoved all of this into the cracks of my days or I did it with my kids literally hanging on me. Sure, the house was a little dirtier and the mountains of laundry were a little higher, but I wasn't crying over spilled milk anymore. And that was just the start.

None of the items I crossed off were worthy of front-page headlines. And yet, prioritizing that list changed my life because it helped me put myself on my *own* list. It didn't just give me back time, it gave me back *me*. Little by little, doing *something* on my list reminded me of who I was and pointed me toward the breadcrumbs of who I wanted to be. Because the point of the list was exploration, not completion, I was allowed to be bad at things—it was okay to fail, it was acceptable to be mediocre. Doing so not only showed me that it was possible to grow outside of my

---

[1]My community now knows this list as the *Do Something List*, aka DSL.

perfectionistic, all-or-nothing (mostly nothing by then) tendencies, it also weirdly gave me more confidence.

That list turned into a years-long experiment of what it looks like to progress for progress's sake. I began sharing about this idea and my experiences with it online, and eventually interviewed others about their own journeys as well on my new amateur podcast, *About Progress*. It was another venture I was allowed to be bad at just as long as I was trying.

For the first time in my adult life, I was working on my personal growth for richer, truer reasons—not to meet prescriptions or achieve accolades, and not because I *should* be, but because I was *choosing* to. In the process, I was finding "Monica" again in ways that felt like a sort of reclamation.

Bubbles to Bowels

The early fruits of this reclamation became clear as I encountered a real-life drama, one that far exceeded my performance with spilled solutions. Instead of bubbles, this spectacle involved bowels. Yes, bowels.

A few years after that incident with the bubbles, I was due to have our fourth child—another boy. Thanks to years of scraping together our pennies, we were finally able to embark on a "cheap" kitchen renovation leading up to his birth. Since we were trying to do as much as we could ourselves, and because we had no idea what we were doing, a lot went wrong. *A lot.*

As most renovation stories go, the timeline and budget doubled. The people we originally hired for a few big things made costly mistakes, the kinds where you fail every inspection and have to rip out what they did and start all over. We figured this out on December 23, and our baby was due February 3. Our kitchen was an empty hole with everything stripped down to the studs. There were no walls, no insulation, no piping, nothing. Oh, and no contractor or hired teams to finish the job.

Our home was 1,200 square feet, so the "renovation" (really, a travesty) disrupted every part of our lives. Our single bathroom was our only source of water, and its tiny countertop where I tried to cook with the instant pot and electric griddle placed *just so*. Thanks to our laundry appliances being removed as part of the renovation, Brad had to haul our giant laundry bags to and from the laundromat late at night after work to spare my now heavily pregnant body the duty. Every inch of our home was covered in a fine layer of dust, no matter what I did.

And we were going to have to bring a newborn home to *all* that, now with no end in sight?! There's a picture from this time that Brad likes to tease me with from Christmas day that year. I'm sitting on the floor, slumped against the couch, belly bursting my non-maternity jacket to the seams, my face drained of all life and energy. I was the kind of "stressed and depleted" you can't hide.

Thankfully, *one* woman answered my plea for help on a random local mom Facebook group, saying her handyman husband (also a certified contractor) would be able to work with us. In the month before our baby's birth, this man fixed all the others' mistakes and got us to the drywall stage, something I'll forever be grateful for. We were able to get floors in and drywall, too. Our Ikea cabinets were delivered just in time for us to begin to assemble.

My baby was a few days overdue—a first for me—and we were set to head in to get induced as my prior births had been scary fast. (I did *not* want to accidentally give birth in the aisle of a Safeway grocery store.) The day before our induction appointment, our only toilet in the house started pumping sewer water into our home, and then our only car got stuck at the mechanic's. I hired a plumber, we borrowed a car, and Brad's parents kindly watched the big kids so we could go and have a baby.

After a smooth labor and a short hospital stay, we brought him home. I remember sitting on our couch holding his warm body, stroking his white-blonde hair, admiring his perfect lips, and never feeling more grateful for walls and floors. It didn't matter that we didn't have a kitchen with running water, cabinets, or counters. We were warm, and we were safe. (Also, we had a working toilet again, hallelujah!)

Brad went back to work a few days later and my mom flew in to sleep on our pullout couch, helping me with the big kids so I could recover from birth—aka paint cabinet doors in the garage while the baby napped. At nine days old—Valentine's Day—my mom and I could both see something wasn't quite right with my baby.

He seemed like he was in pain, but not the normal newborn gas kind of pain. His little tummy would scrunch up hard, just like his face, and he would wail like he was getting stabbed. He wouldn't eat, couldn't sleep, and he occasionally spit up electric-green fluid instead of the typically sweet-smelling breast milk. As the day wore on, I felt a growing foreboding feeling, despite the fact that his symptoms were dissipating and he got a decent night's sleep.

The next morning, I called my pediatrician with my concerns and she wisely sent us to the hospital for testing. While kind, the radiologist told me her X-ray showed our baby was fine. I insisted they try other tests, a kind of boldness I rarely embody in a medical setting. The third—and most invasive—test was ordered and quickly prepared: an endoscopy, where a camera was inserted into our baby's throat and down into his gastrointestinal tract.

The moment the camera met its mark, the doctor became urgent. She finished the test quickly, rushed a nurse off with instructions, and gravely told me, "Your baby's bowels are twisted and he needs surgery right away." I asked her if he would die if we didn't do it immediately. She nodded and firmly said, "Yes."

While I waited to be escorted to the emergency room (ER), I held my baby for what could be the last time. He was calm now, his pain somehow abated. He couldn't nurse because of the surgery, but he wasn't eager to anyway—his little tummy was already full with bile squeezed up from his twisted intestines. I called Brad and told him to come as fast as he could from San Francisco. I took a few pictures of my little one, some with my face scrunched right up next to his so I could always remember the two of us, together.

The next few hours were a blur, starting with a spectacle in the ER room while they prepped our baby for surgery. I can see it all now in a sort of haze: needles struggling to find tiny, dehydrated veins, heated doctors shouting at each other over protocols, me begging God for a miracle, and a pediatric anesthesiologist performing one. Brad swooped in the minute before they were to escort our little one away. He got to hold our baby, saying his own sort of potential goodbye. Together, we experienced the feelings of seeing your newborn taken behind doors and walls you can't follow, of the worries plaguing your waiting on the other side.

The next time I saw my newborn was in the pediatric intensive care unit. His face was puffy, his lips were dry—but he was alive. I counted the number of tubes coming from him and the monitors tracking every vital. And I fell into a hesitant relief.

Six days later—much sooner than they thought we would—we brought him home again. My mom had thankfully extended her stay and had worked on assembling the cabinetry, alongside a kind neighbor and the handyman, who had come back to assist in our time of need.

I was back again in a dusty home and a kitchen with no cabinets, no counters, and no laundry, sink, and faucet, but now with four children under my care, including a baby recovering from a life-saving surgery. My mom needed to head home, and Brad had no choice but to return to his long hours at work. Again, I was the only one. I had to do it all. It was all on me.

And yet, this time I felt like I could.

Though I was stressed, exhausted, and overwhelmed—I felt like *myself.* I was still "Monica." I was capable, kind, and persistent. I was creative, smart, and ambitious. I was calm, thoughtful, and hard-working.

I could meet these challenges. I could do what needed to be done. I could show up. Not just for my people and this difficult time, but for myself, too.

Why? Why and how could I do this when the stakes were so much bigger, so much weightier than another spilled bottle of bubbles? It was all thanks to recent years of learning who I was again and putting myself on my own list.

Only the Beginning

When I came home from the hospital for the second time with the same newborn, I didn't know it yet but this was only the beginning. It was just the start of me learning how to reclaim my life, choose progress over perfection, and feel like myself.

Fast forward eight years later, I can honestly tell you that most of my life looks the same. I now have five children, many of whom have special needs. I am still the primary parent, caring for our kids and home in the many mundane (but vital!) ways running a household requires. Money remains limited. I deal with stress, insecurity, and occasionally depressive and anxious seasons.

However, while my life looks mostly the same, it *feels* completely different. Because in even better, deeper, and more practical ways than after my baby almost died, I am "Monica."

I credit that not only to how I reclaimed my life outside of perfectionism but also to how doing so gradually expanded to how I do habits.

There is much more to say on that last bit (obviously!), but I'll leave it now with this truth: while unique to me, my tale is a collective one.

A Call to Rebel

From bubbles to bowels, we all face hardships in our lives. They come, they go, they stick around. The only way to get through life and not be lost to it all is to reclaim our right to a life that reflects the woman living it. When we feel centered and supported, we can be ready, willing, and able to show up for ourselves, our people, and our responsibilities. Because at long last, we count ourselves as one of them.

Women can't show up as the leaders they are if they continue to follow the perfection-bound prescriptions passed down to us. So to truly begin, we have to do something that might initially feel shocking: rebel.

TAKEAWAYS: I share my own origin story of learning to reclaim my life, choose progress over perfection, and prioritize myself again. Thanks to doing so, I was able to *be* myself during hard times. This work eventually translated to habits—stay tuned for the next chapter!

TAKE THOUGHT: When was a time that you forfeited yourself for your responsibilities? How did perfectionistic models of being a woman create that experience for you?

TAKE ACTION: Ask yourself, "Do I think I only have two choices: me or my responsibilities?" Consider what would be different for you if you made space for *and* instead of *or.*

NOTE: For more (printables, recommended books, complementary podcast episodes, etc.), remember to check out the free and included Sticky Habit resources, available online at https://stickyhabitsbook.com/resources:

Chapter 2

The Two-Word, Number One Reason Why Women Must Do Habits Differently

Learn: Why habit methods can't be gender neutral, and how women's lives are different from men's lives in one significant (well-studied) way

Thanks to reconnecting with myself and my rising passion for personal growth outside of perfectionism, I was making great strides in every area of my life. Until I hit a plateau. Basically, I wasn't sleeping.

It wasn't that I was naturally energetic and didn't need much sleep. It was because nighttime hours were used for working on my podcast and occasional attempts at "self-care." I likely would have continued in my night owl ways if it weren't for some good old-fashioned vanity that pushed me to acknowledge I could not go on sleeping the way I was.

My friend—a wonderful photographer—had taken our family photos the year prior while I was pregnant and admittedly sleeping better than normal. (Pregnancy fatigue will do that to you.) She did so again, creating magical shots of our young family, now including the sweetest seven-month-old healthy baby boy. When I got the pictures back, I loved them—except for one thing: I looked . . . old. As in, significantly older than my 32 years, and much older than our pictures almost exactly one year prior.

I knew right away that it was because of my lack of sleep. I couldn't blame the baby who was sleeping fine by that point, typically waking up just once a night. But I wasn't. I was up doing *all* the things late, late into the night. My early-morning workouts certainly weren't helping! Throw it all together and it was clear my lack of sleep was taking a toll. One I could literally see.

I was no longer able to coast on the buzz of re-prioritizing myself again. I simply *had* to sleep better. But, this also was true for other long-forgotten habits. I needed to plan out my days again and journaling was certain to help calm my racing mind—just to name a couple.

Knowing myself again was one thing, but now I needed to learn how to support that "self" on the daily.

But, I thought I wasn't a "habit person." I had been there, done that, aspiring to have the right habits in the right ways (read: perfect), and those aspirations not only didn't stick they also hurt me on the way out. But, here I was, hurting in other ways by *not* trying.

So, could I dare? Could I apply my newfound knowledge of progress over perfection to the elusive world of habit formation? Could I become a "habit person?" The answer was yes. And the answer is *still* yes—I am a habit person now; just not the kind I originally thought I had to be. Finding that answer took several years.

A Shared Plateau

Some of the bestselling books in my adult life have been about habits. I've read them all. My copies are heavily dog-eared and highlighted, and they are sitting on my office bookshelf this very minute.

These are books that I dove into while trying to correct my face . . . I mean, my sleep. They contained the most up-to-date methods on what habit formation should look like. It felt weirdly exciting to be returning to my type-A roots and to attempt to work on habits again. I devoured these bestsellers, then rushed to apply what I learned with great anticipation.

Only to fall flat on my face.

These methods required a level of perfection I found near impossible to sustain. I never seemed to hold onto the "consistency" they described. The few habits I was able to maintain demanded such a concerted effort that I quickly fell behind in other responsibilities. No matter how sincerely I tried, my new habits weren't sticking.

If it weren't for my overall pursuit of "progress over perfection," I would have quit right then and there, convinced by more evidence that I was a failure. Instead, I chose to keep an open mind, to revisit the books and their principles, to try again, and to do so in a playful way, curious about what helped my habits actually stick.

This is when you'd see a movie montage of a few years of work—me reading, me trying, me failing, me trying again. Results were decidedly mixed, but I wasn't ready to hang my habit hat.

During this time of personal experimentation, something unexpected happened. I began coaching other women who needed to work on habits, too. Despite my hesitations with the coaching industry, I knew that I could confidently guide fellow women to rediscover who they are, help them learn to separate their sense of self from their outcomes, and make progress in their lives outside the pendulum swings of perfectionism.

The women I worked with were making incredible strides. They saw themselves differently, they were trying and growing in new ways, but . . . just like me, they began to hit plateaus.

They similarly discovered that knowing themselves was one thing, but *feeling* like themselves on a day-to-day basis was quite another. Their rediscovered knowledge of self had to have practical application, the kind of daily support that made that "self" possible. My clients needed habits, too.

They desired to:

- Feel more like themselves
- Have more energy
- Improve their relationships
- Deepen their spiritual practice
- Improve their sleep
- Have time for interests and hobbies
- Create order in their day-to-day lives

And to do any one of those things, it was undeniably clear—they had to have consistent habits.

In my pursuit to be a more credible coach, I had submersed myself into a 300-day coaching certification program called Optimize (now known as Heroic). I was so happy to discover my training included additional education on habits, with information largely pulled directly from the well-established habit experts lining my bookshelf. With this deepened "know-how" under my belt, I confidently offered up these methods to my coaching clients.

To my surprise, they quickly grew frustrated. My clients would apply the methods with exactness, only to find that while some parts would work, most would not. Their habits weren't sustainable without tremendous effort, the kind we quickly learned came at a cost in energy, mental capacity, and (ironically) consistency. It was undeniable: even with these most up-to-date methods, all of my clients were struggling to create habits that stick.

I knew these women well. They weren't weak. They weren't lazy. They didn't lack discipline and willpower. And seeing their struggles refuted the doubt lingering in my own mind: neither was I.

I was forced to either blame us all, or to take a bigger step back and truly analyze the methods we were applying. Because if they were so "good," why weren't they good enough for the women I was coaching?

I sat with this puzzle for some time. I see now that the answer had been building under the surface for years, but in the moment it felt like my own personal eureka: the books we were learning from and the methods we were struggling to apply were all written and designed by men.

Unintended Male Bias

That last sentence might be giving you pause. Maybe it feels too feminist—"Why do we blame the patriarchy for everything???" Maybe it doesn't feel feminist enough—"Women can do anything men can do!!!"

To both of these pushbacks, I say, "I agree with you."

These are Good Men with Great Methods. (I'll refer to them as *GMGMs* for short, *habit bros*, or *bro self-help*. Respectfully, I promise.) I can't discount the service GMGMs have provided for the world and how their concepts have helped so many—women included—to make significant changes in their lives. I also firmly believe that women have the same potential as their male counterparts to grow, change, and make a difference in the world at large.

It's just that we don't have the same opportunity. That's a bold statement, but it's one I'll explain.

My realization that these methods were authored solely by men is shared not to dismiss or criticize them. Instead, I seek to validate the many, many women who have failed in applying their approaches, only to blame themselves. They were missing that the methods weren't designed for them to begin with.

How do I know this?

Just like I know my wide iPhone wasn't designed for my slight hand, nor were my electronic devices trained to recognize requests from my higher-pitched voice. Just like I know that the medicine I may need to take for my heart one day wasn't studied with my female hormones despite heart disease being the number one killer for women. Just like I know that if I get in a car accident, the seat belt was likely not created for my female body.[1]

In her somewhat depressing book, *Invisible Women*, Caroline Criado Perez shares about the great gender gap in research, much of which uses men as the given baseline in everything from conducting studies to product design. In a world fabricated largely by men with other men in mind, everything from companies to cities have been and continue to be negligent in considering women. Even public bus systems failed to study women's transportation patterns and needs, despite women acting as their main users. This negligence ranges from eliminating women as factors completely, to making them the minority of consideration. And this is true for products just as it's true for policies.

I found myself grinding my teeth while reading, but I had to pause and really let it sink in when Criado Perez wrote, "Failing to include the perspective of women is a huge driver of unintended male bias that attempts (often in good faith) to pass itself off as 'gender neutral.'"

This, to me, encapsulates the main problem of men being the primary (if only) leaders in habit formation. The GMGMs are not intentionally trying to leave us out; they simply forget that our lives are different from theirs.

---

[1] Caroline Criado Perez, *Invisible Women: Data Bias in a World Designed for Men* (Abrams Press, 2019).

This unintentional bias slips into the bestselling, male-authored habit books when you consider a few things.[2]

The first is how these methods were created over years of the author's own pursuit of cracking the habit code. Their findings were both informed by and applied in their male lives, those absent of the elements that make women's lives different. That doesn't discount their findings, but it does prevent those findings from being gender neutral.

Another piece of unintentional bias is the actual research. Like me, most of these men aren't professional researchers or social scientists, so they didn't conduct control-driven studies that were divided by gender. Gender likely wasn't a high consideration, if at all.[3]

Instead of formalized studies, almost all of these habit gurus based their "proof of concept" on case studies that were largely (and I mean, almost entirely) specific to men. If there are references to women, they are mostly passing snippets, largely anonymous, with just one woman (*maybe* two or three if we're lucky) getting a full chapter dedicated to her as the main character. In one of the most popular of these habit books, the ratio of male-to-female stories shared is 7:1. Other references to the general public are worded to be more gender neutral, like "business leaders" and "athletes," without stating their sex. I'd put good money on what gender the majority of references actually point to.

While we can see a few women featured, we don't know what lengths they had to go to in order to locate women who successfully used their methods, and whether the ones they did uncover

[2] I won't be super specific about which authors do which things, as I truly am not out to attack their work. My desire is to build off of what they do well and use what can apply to us as women, while also pointing out what they lack and filling those gaps. I still recommend reading these books and you'll find them listed in the online resources, among others.

[3] For the very few that did conduct research of their methods, none divided their case studies into separate groupings of men and women. This makes it impossible to distinguish if there was a gender gap in the efficacy of their methods.

were in the minority compared to other women who tried and failed. We don't even know if these case studies are based on specific, real people—or if they are composites of clients they worked with or even made up. (Both scenarios are common in self-help books, I'm sorry to say.) Furthermore, even valid conglomerations may have been assigned a female name in an effort to be inclusive because the authors sincerely assumed their work was applicable to both genders. (It's not.)

Intended Female Bias

I acknowledge that, like almost all of these men, I am also not a social scientist who performed gender-divided, controlled studies. However, what I will teach here is not based on just my lived experience. I have been a habits and identity coach for over eight years with well over 1,000 women as coaching clients and students who have applied my teachings.

The book you are reading right now *is* biased. From its origins of me getting curious with habits, to applying tweaks first in my life and then those of my clients, students, and podcast listeners—99% of whom are women—it is biased on every level. While I'm sure men who are facing more of a survival period in their lives or find themselves taking on more care-taking roles could find much, if not all, of my method applicable to them, they were not specifically considered. I acknowledge this bias not as a detriment to my work, but as a strength, especially for women who are ready to rebel against the prescriptions that were never designed for them.

I also acknowledge that even then, I didn't start from scratch. After all, these habit experts are GMGMs. W.I. Thomas wrote, "Every idea is a descendent of another." In that spirit, I will teach you what I learned from the methods that came before me, extracting what is wise and applicable to us as women and building off of what they have to offer, all while filling in the unintended gaps that led many women to fail in full application of them in the first place.

And that brings us to the main question, the one that either validates or tears down the whole foundation of my work: ***Are women's lives different from men's lives? And if so, what does that have to do with habits?***

COVID-19 Revealed a Preexisting Truth

I read *Invisible Women* halfway through 2020, the year of the COVID-19 pandemic. It's also the year I had my eureka moment, and now it's so obvious why. As deeply as all of our lives were affected by the shutdowns, women's lives were affected in more deep and lasting ways.

My life was one of them. The pandemic forced a hasty move from our home in California to my parents' basement in Utah. This was in large part to ensure our daughter, who was newly diagnosed with autism, had access to needed services. All of my kids struggled greatly during this period. I did my best to manage their needs, while also homeschooling three out of the four children, working remotely part-time, and managing a stressful renovation of an old home (read: money pit) we purchased 30 minutes away. My husband, Brad, became severely depressed. He had navigated waves with his mental health for years, but that storm became an all-consuming tsunami that threatened to pull him down to the deepest, darkest waters. I feared he would never reemerge.

With our family's ship already on a rocky sea, the giant swells of all the pressures, all the stress, and all the unknowns of living in a worldwide pandemic threatened to swallow us whole. And it was me who had to step up as the main navigator and captain.

I paint this picture not because I believe we had it worse than most, but because I *know* we had it better than most. If my family's life was in upheaval while I took the brunt of it, then imagine how so many women were navigating even deeper, more treacherous waters.

The UN Women organization released an early report in November of 2020 of the effects of COVID-19 on households.

Their findings showed that while all "unpaid care and domestic work" had risen thanks to more people being at home, women were carrying "the lion's share."[4]

I saw these demands play out with the women I serve. Many were forced to continue their full-time jobs while also overseeing their kids' virtual schooling—an impossible feat—battling both constant guilt and increased sensory input. Some had to quit their jobs to manage the sudden influx of near-constant needs of their home life and struggling children. Others lost family members to COVID, layering grief on their already heavy lives. Some became caretakers for their elderly parents. And a few lost their jobs, or their spouses did. Even the "typical" woman found her already-heavy-but-normal responsibilities blown out of proportion, her daily tasks becoming a tempest of to-dos that overwhelmed even the most capable of women. And women did it all while isolated from their already insufficient support systems.

And yet, women did what needed to be done. Why? Because it really, really mattered.

From the UN Women report:

> *The COVID-19 global crisis has exposed the fact that the world's economies and our daily lives are made possible by the unpaid care work of women and girls, which is often invisible and under-appreciated . . . . Unpaid care is a key dimension of pandemic responses—enabling both well-being, education and income-generation, particularly given homeschooling, elder vulnerability and work-from-home arrangements.*[5]

This is what we do as women: we show up.

We always have. It's just that most people didn't see us.

---

[4] "Whose Time to Care: Unpaid Care and Domestic Work During Covid-19," UN Women Organization, 2020. https://data.unwomen.org/sites/default/files/inline-files/Whose-time-to-care-brief_0.pdf?utm.

[5] Ibid.

Invisible Labor

While the pandemic highlighted the extreme loads women carry, many smart people already knew that.

The disparity of caretaking women bear has been a subject of great interest with decades-long research ranging in fields from economics, to gender studies, to social science.[6] It became *my* interest when I realized why women using the "habit bro methods" were doomed to fail.

There was something different about us as women that I could no longer ignore: our lives are different from men's lives. Hormones alone could act as a single, but vast, explanation for the differences between men and women. But, I tracked that this disparity came down to something both so pragmatic and complex—the two-word number one reason why women must do habits differently: **invisible labor.**

Invisible labor is the literal and mental/emotional labor performed to keep homes, communities, and institutions running that is largely undervalued, unpaid or underpaid, and unseen.[7]

Think: childcare, eldercare, home management, or any other caretaking role. But with those, also think of the sheer volume of both internal toil and external work that make any of those priorities possible, from knowing that Eloise needs a new pair of socks, to tracking who has to be where and when, to being the one solely responsible for replacing all toilet paper rolls and keeping the toilet paper stocked, too.

[6] In the online resources available to you, I share a whole list of papers, articles, and books to explore on this subject.
[7] My definition is a conglomeration of many out there.

Who performs the vast majority of invisible labor? Women.

Research shows that this is true for every country on earth, transcending politics, religion, and social structures—women take on the majority of invisible labor tasks.[8] From the accomplished entrepreneur to the super stay-at-home mom, it's women who are the default person in charge of caretaking in all its forms. That's even true in the workspaces: Who plans your work parties? Who buys the cards for the birthdays? Who makes sure the workroom is stocked with coffee or extra forks?

You would think that in modern times the division of labor would balance out between women and men. You'd be wrong.

Some "fun" stats:

- Ninety percent of participants for a study performed in the United States of married or partnered mothers[9] "reported taking exclusive responsibility for household tasks."[10]
- Married moms in the United States "spend nearly double the time on housework and childcare than American fathers do."[11]
- Almost 90% of study participants "said they bore sole responsibility for organizing their family's schedules," while "70% said they were the 'captain' of their ship and routinely completed and assigned household tasks."[12]

These statistics are true for women whether or not they work outside the home, even if they're partnered, and regardless of if

---

[8] "Whose Time to Care."

[9] This part is important because that means they'd likely have a man in their lives.

[10] L. Ciciolla and S. S. Luthar, "Invisible Household Labor and Ramifications for Adjustment: Mothers as Captains of Households," *Sex Roles* 81, no. 3 (2019): 467–486. https://doi.org/10.1007/s11199-018-10.1-x.

[11] Claire Cain Miller, "How Society Pays When Women's Work Is Unpaid." *New York Times*, 22 February 2016. https://www.nytimes.com/2016/02/23/upshot/how-society-pays-when-womens-work-is-unpaid.html?_r=0.

[12] A.C. Weeks and L. Ruppanner, "A Typology of US Parents' Mental Loads: Core and Episodic Cognitive Labor," *Journal of Marriage and Family* 87, no. 3 (2025): 966–989. https://doi.org/10.1111/jomf.13057.

children reside at home. I've seen its effects take hold of my clients who are grandmothers in retirement just as much as clients who are young female working professionals without children, stay-at-home mothers of several children, and women who don't have children in the home for one reason or another.

The Heavy Mental Load

For those of us lucky to live in more egalitarian households—with supportive male partners and other contributing household members (e.g., children/grandparents) participating in caretaking tasks—that last stat on women predominately being in charge at home is really fascinating as it describes the weight of the *mental load* that comes with invisible labor. Let's say your husband will make dinner, or do the laundry, or take kids where they need to be, or sign the children up for sports; even then, you are statistically more likely to be the one *directing* that work, which still requires mental labor to manage. The toil and toll of that load cannot be downplayed; it cannot be discounted.

This mental load was featured heavily in a fantastic book by Eve Rodsky, *Fair Play*, where she uses her years as a corporate business lawyer to highlight how home/family management typically focuses on the tasks—who does what—but not who manages and assigns those tasks. Rodsky translates a business organizational framework to the home. She says there are three phases to any task completion: conception, planning, and execution (CPE).[13] If you are only being assigned to execute a task, you're failing to fully acknowledge the work involved in conceiving of it and planning it out as well. So, even if other household members are carrying

[13] Eve Rodsky, *Fair Play: A Game-Changing Solution for When You Have Too Much to Do (and More Life to Live)* (Penguin Random House, 2021).

more of the visible labor involved with carework, we still fail to see who mostly manages the mental labor (the conceiving and planning) of making that task possible: women.

The mental load alone accounts for a great deal of women's time and energy. This time is super difficult to quantify by researchers, but one has noted that mothers "manage 7 in 10 mental tasks," so that's 71% of a typical home's required "thinking labor."[14]

If you're unsure if invisible labor is something you deal with, please factor in the mental load.

With her research in 17 countries on the gender disparity of home labor—including mentally—Eve Rodsky found that women underreport the loads they carry and men overreport,[15] making it difficult at first for her to accurately piece together what was happening within partnerships. Women had a hard time even tracking what they do because they're like fish swimming in the sea, not recognizing that it's water they're swimming in.

Luckily, Rodsky discovered *one* defining question that really set the wheels in motion, showing women just how much they carried compared to their male partners, both literally and mentally: "How does mustard get in your fridge?"

Replace mustard with any condiment. This simple question does not entail a simple answer. The mustard got there because someone tracked the flavor preferences of all members of the family, someone noted which were in stock in the fridge and which were running low, someone added mustard to a shopping list, someone got it from the store, and someone brought it back and put it where it needed to go.

---

[14] Ciciolla and Luthar, "Invisible Household Labor and Ramifications for Adjustment: Mothers as Captains of Households."
https://researchportal.bath.ac.uk/en/publications/a-typology-of-us-parents-mental-loads-core-and-episodic-cognitive/?utm_.
[15] https://www.youtube.com/watch?v=cKNEKcrVFYk.

If that "someone" is not carrying around the family's preferences nor tracking what's in or what's out, they will likely arrive back home with the wrong mustard, if they got any at all. And, as Eve says it, "Little Johnny won't eat his protein with Dijon . . . ." Women know the frustration of their husband coming home with the wrong mustard when it's so *obvious* to them which kind is actually needed. This is why they often end up doing most things themselves, because it's "easier."

So, how does mustard get in your fridge? And how does answering that question reveal to you the mental waters you are swimming in?

Invisible Labor's Invisible Influence on the Economy

It's easy for society to dismiss what it requires to manage our institutions—from families to communities—because we have long found it easy to dismiss women. But, caretaking in all its forms is indeed "work" and it is essential to all other "visible" forms of work to thrive. Without invisible labor, society's very foundations would crumble, not to mention our family calendars.

Despite unpaid labor not being counted toward the gross domestic product, it is incredibly valuable work. On this, Caroline Criado Perez writes, "Women's unpaid work is the work that society depends on, and it is work from which society as a whole benefits." Eve Rodsky's work on better balancing the load women carry in the home is not to downplay what this work entails. Indeed, Rodsky is pushing for us all to value home life as "the most important organization on earth."

The *New York Times* once calculated just how essential this unpaid, invisible labor is. In 2019, they conducted a study and slapped a number on what they estimated all the unseen tasks for carework and home management would be worth if they were hired out. That total was revealed as a $10.9 trillion a year industry.[16] But frustratingly, even this number significantly undervalues this kind of labor as it was based off of the minimum federal wage of $7.25/hour, a number that hasn't been updated since 2009. Even this calculated number reflects how we deem caretaking work as more menial and less valuable in nature.

The UN Women organization supported those findings though, reporting in 2020 that "16.4 billion hours are spent on unpaid care work every day—the equivalent of 2 billion people working 8 hours per day without pay. The actual value of this work amounts to 9% of global GDP—equivalent to USD 11 trillion."[17]

Women's lives are different from men's lives.

Perhaps you live in a home where you are more seen. Perhaps in your culture, your church, and your neighborhood the unpaid labor you perform is greatly valued. Then I would tell you a few things: first, good! Second, you would be in the minority. Third, valuing this work is one thing, but acknowledging that it changes the way you can show up as compared to your male counterparts is another.

This is where I need to tell you what invisible labor has to do with habit formation.

TAKEAWAYS: Popular habit formation methods were designed to be gender neutral, but women's lives are different from men's lives. This is largely due to invisible labor being predominately carried by women. Invisible labor is the literal and mental/emotional labor performed to keep homes, communities, and institutions running that is largely undervalued, unpaid or underpaid, and unseen.

---

[16] "Women's Unpaid Labor Is Worth $10.9 Trillion." *New York Times*, 5 March 2020. Reported in summaries of the *New York Times* analysis.

[17] "Whose Time to Care."

TAKE THOUGHT: In what ways is your life different from the men you know? How does mustard get into your fridge?

TAKE ACTION: Pay attention to the mental load you carry thanks to invisible labor, and how it affects you.

NOTE: For more (printables, recommended books, complementary podcast episodes, etc.), remember to check out the free and included Sticky Habit resources, available online at https://stickyhabitsbook.com/resources:

Chapter 3

How "Habit Bro Methods" Set Women Up to Fail

Learn: How invisible labor affects women's ability to maintain habits, and why GMGMs set women up to fail with their gendered methods

In my experience and in surveying my community, women experience more failure when applying popular habit formation methods. This is what likely brought you to this book. You may be tired of failing your habits, but aren't you also tired of blaming yourself?

I believe that it's time that women stop blaming themselves for their supposed lack of self-discipline, low motivation, and poor self-control. It's time that we actually take a look at the methods and how *they* fail women, not the other way around.

While these are Good Men with Great Methods (GMGMs), thanks to the well-intentioned, but gendered way they were studied, created, and written, they are missing something essential: women's lives are different from men's lives.

How is this true with forming habits?

I see it comes down to a few main categories. Thanks to the invisible labor we carry, women:

- Experience more interruptions
- Require more flexibility
- Lack predictable circumstances
- Have less time, energy, and support

Let me briefly break each of these down, and then I'll connect it all back to why the GMGMs don't work well for women.

Women Experience More Interruptions

Invisible labor greatly centers on caretaking tasks—in other words, people. Because of this, women get interrupted all the freaking time. You may think, "Ah, yes, children do that." And while you're right, you're also missing husbands, coworkers, neighbors, schools, and more. Caretaking isn't just about children—it's about *everyone*. This is something I saw time and time again with the clients under my care.

Beth was a grandma in her 60s, employed outside the home while also recovering from very intense cancer treatments. I worked with her to gain the habit of resting (yes, resting is a habit!). She was desperate to prioritize reading again, something that enabled both her brain and body to relax. We selected "after dinner cleanup" as a good time of day for her to read. Beth set out to implement her new habit, starting with a 10-minute reading session on her recliner right after wiping off her kitchen counter. Easy enough, right?

When I checked in on how her progress was going, Beth responded, "Monica, it's been a lot harder than I thought it would be." Habit fails should elicit curiosity (more on this later in the book), so I asked Beth a bunch of questions. It turned out that nearly every time she sat down and cracked open her book, Beth's husband would ask her a question, seek directions on where something was located, or simply strike up a conversation.

Interruptions are easily one of the biggest obstacles women face as they seek to gain their own consistent habits. Yet rather than blame the interruptions, they blame themselves.

Women Require More Flexibility

Invisible labor requires a great deal of flexibility from us as women.

Caretaking responsibilities—from laundry to meals—tend to be more urgent in nature. For example, you shouldn't ignore the washer signaling completion of its cycle if you don't want musty clothes in need of a second washing, potentially followed by a moldy appliance. These urgency-bound tasks, especially when coupled with interruptions, require us as women to be flexible with what we do in a day. There may be more tasks piled on in a second or we have to switch directions all together, which often leads to us abandoning our well-laid plans. Without our flexibility to respond, others' needs will go unmet.

Writing this reminds me of my most recent postpartum season and my attempt to complete a "simple" 20-minute workout video. Soon after starting my squats, my baby woke up a few minutes into his nap. I paused the video and took the time to rock him back to sleep. I began my workout again, but had to pause it once more when I noticed a text from the pest control guy saying he was arriving in 30 minutes to take care of a black widow problem we were having. I hurriedly tidied as much as I could before he came, then welcomed the serviceman and talked through the issue. While he worked, I tried to get back to my video, only to have the baby wake up again. I chose a mini "reset" for him, giving the baby a bit more time and activity before a final attempt at his much-needed nap. Once he was finally back in his crib, I returned to my video and pressed play, but then I got a call from the school about needing to pay for lunches our kids weren't supposed to have ("It's free, Mom!"). I began the video once more, and a few minutes in, the baby made it known that he was *not* going to sleep, thank you very much.

The reasonable side of me said, "Enough is enough—your workout is over for today." I paused the video for the final time at 14 minutes in. Then, I stopped my Apple watch tracking the time all along and laughed out loud at what I saw on the timestamp: 2.5 hours!!! 2.5 hours to complete 14 minutes of my "simple" 20-minute workout video. I admit that I felt both frustrated and defeated—*why even try?*

That sentiment is shared by so many women. They seek to create supportive habits in their lives only to have their efforts foiled by demanding responsibilities requiring their immediate attention. Women find it's simply easier to throw in the towel than to persist in what feels akin to acting out a scene from a comedy, but not the romantic kind. This "hilarity" only increases when we try to plug in self-help prescriptions that rely on a predictable sort of existence, one absent of the flexibility that is demanded of women.

Women Lack Predictable Circumstances

I don't know a single woman who can count on a day going even remotely close to plan. This again has been true for my clients across all of life's spectrum of seasons, including children or no children in the home.

One of my very favorite coaching clients was a woman in her late 40s named Taryn who, despite desperately wanting them, was unable to have children. Her days were filled working as a virtual assistant, as the neighborhood's piano teacher, and as the world's best aunt. These duties all combined with her exhaustive responsibilities at church and at home, making Taryn's life both busy and unpredictable. One of Taryn's greatest issues was getting too caught up in all the urgent tasks she had to do each day, with very little time to devote to her own interests or to even take a real break.

Fake breaks came up too often after dinner when her energy was low, typically resulting in scroll sessions on social media for much longer than felt good to her. When we tried to isolate other times of the day for her to implement what came to be known as

Taryn Time, it was very hard to do so because every single day looked different thanks to her rotating care-based tasks, from piano students to urgent home duties. Even when Taryn had a day planned out, it never—and I mean *never*—matched her intentions.

We can't ignore that our circumstances make it difficult to count on a regular schedule, one where we can predictably do the same habit in the same way at the same time of day, day after day. And then multiply that by 10 for the habits we actually need for *ourselves*, those outside our more urgent responsibilities.

There is hope though: we do have rhythms to our days with already existing habits that create a sort of dependable pattern for new habits to be built on—just not in the ways we were taught. Sit tight to learn more on this in Chapter 8.

Women Have Less Time, Energy, and Support

All of the prior notes build up to a big one: thanks to the nature and the load of the invisible tasks we carry, women have less time, energy, and support.

Author and philanthropist Melinda French Gates has been sounding the alarm bells of the disparity of home labor for years, calling it "one of those hidden root inequities." One of the main reasons she is doing so comes down to time, and how women have less of it than men.

She writes, "On average worldwide, women spend about four and a half hours a day on unpaid domestic work like laundry, child care, and house cleaning, which is more than double what men do."[1] She also notes that in India that daily disparity is six hours for women, with less than one hour a day for men. In many ways, in

[1] Dayna Evans, "Melinda Gates: Unpaid Domestic Labor is a 'Hidden Root Inequity'." *The Cut*, 1 April 2016. https://www.thecut.com/2016/04/melinda-gates-lets-talk-unpaid-domestic-labor.html; Claire Cain Miller, "How Society Pays When Women's Work Is Unpaid." *New York Times*, 22 February 2016. https://www.nytimes.com/2016/02/23/upshot/how-society-pays-when-womens-work-is-unpaid.html?_r=0.

North America we are doing better than other parts of the world in sharing what has long been considered "women's work," from carrying water to caring for children. But, these small gains still don't outpace how much women do that is left unseen, and how much time it takes for women to keep up.

On average, women have less time—time to seek education, to relax, to work, to have hobbies, to nurture friendships, to care for themselves. It's a fact.

It's a direct correlation that we also have less energy. With more to do and less time to do it, women are left more physically and emotionally exhausted. Our stress levels exceed men's, as does our frequency of burnout and poor mental health.[2] Current research is showing that women sacrifice their limited leisure time for sleep. But, even though women slightly sleep more hours on average than men, those hours are "poorer quality sleep" thanks to women who "prioritize family needs, even during sleeping hours."[3]

Finally, women feel less supported. Much of what they carry is not only undervalued compared to paid work, both by society and family members alike, but it's also largely unseen to begin with.

There was recently a trend on social media, "We listen and we don't judge." Participants began their video with that statement, then declared some truths about themselves, followed by "We listen and we don't judge." There was one husband-wife duo taking part in the trend that really stood out to me. While the wife's truths involved things like getting fast food from Chick-fil-A while pretending to do errands or sneaking Botox, every single one of her husband's were about him avoiding helping with housework and caring for the kids.

---

[2] E. Aviv, Y. Waizman, E. Kim, J. Liu, E. Rodsky, and D. Saxbe, "Cognitive Household Labor: Gender Disparities and Consequences for Maternal Mental Health and Wellbeing," *Archives of Women's Mental Health* 28, no. 1 (2025): 5–14. https://doi.org/10.1007/s00737-024-01490-w.

[3] S.A. Burgard and J.A. Ailshire, "Gender and Time for Sleep Among U.S. Adults," *America Sociological Review* 78, no. 1 (2013): 51–69. https://doi.org/10.1177/0003122412472048.

Here are direct quotes from his side:

Exhibit A: "Sometimes I go in the bathroom and hide and pretend to go to the bathroom when I hear the chaos in the house, just so you have to handle it and not me."
Exhibit B: "Sometimes I pretend that I have to fix something downstairs just so I can play video games and have some peace."
Exhibit C: "Sometimes I go in our bedroom at night and pretend to fold laundry while you're downstairs, just so I don't have to help you clean up."
Exhibit D: "Sometimes I ignore you and pretend like I can't hear you in hopes that you'll get so annoyed that you have to repeat it, that you won't ask me to do something again."[4]

Of course, this is just an anecdote of one couple, but it's reflective of many women's reality.

Women often report to me how it's "easier" to simply do everything themselves. Since they're already carrying the conception and planning stages of most tasks, it's easier to execute when doing otherwise requires nagging partners and kids to do their part, then fixing those tasks when they're not done well, if at all.

What Are GMGMs Getting Wrong?

If we can understand that women experience more interruptions, require more flexibility, lack dependable predictable circumstances, and have less time, energy, and support, then **what are traditional habit formation methods (GMGMs) getting wrong**?

First, they are not *all* wrong *all* the time. There are principles that transcend our shared-but-gendered experiences in the world,

[4] https://www.instagram.com/p/DCy7qZnxlqH/. My husband's reaction to this interaction: "Is this man still alive?"

and those are elements I built my method on (small habits and habit stacking, I'm looking at you).

In general, there are two big and important ways the habit bro methods don't work for many women:

- They are too reliant on willpower.
- They are too reliant on predictability.

GMGMs Are Too Reliant on Willpower

Another word for willpower? Energy. I'm talking both the physical and mental/emotional kind. With all that comes with the invisible labor they carry, women are rightfully exhausted.

Tonia was one of them, a capable woman in her late 40s who wanted to return to daily dedicated time to her art practice. She came to me hoping to re-prioritize her creativity, but her expectations were low—not of me, but of herself. Her art practice was a habit she used to have for years while raising her four oldest boys, and one that provided a daily touchpoint to herself amidst all the intense responsibilities she bore. But this practice fell to the wayside when Tonia stepped up as caretaker for her elderly in-laws on top of homeschooling her youngest of five, a child with some special needs born many years later than her older siblings. The stress was so high for a few years that Tonia lived in a permanent "survival state," with each day looking like a full-on sprint from sunrise to sunset.

Tonia's in-laws passed away and there was a great period of both grief and readjustment back to "normal life." Now a year later, Tonia was at a loss for why she hadn't returned to regularly investing in her creativity, something her soul *needed*. She doubted her own willpower as she kept intending to set aside the time, could do so for a day or two, but then the habit would drop alongside Tonia's faith in herself. She thought it was realistic for her to devote at least an hour per day to art since she did that in the past. She wasn't working at the moment nor caring for her in-laws, so she technically had more time. Why couldn't she make this habit stick? Her inability to do so made Tonia feel weak and foolish.

In our time together, Tonia learned a great deal about habit formation, but she learned even more about herself. I helped Tonia see what was really on her plate. Sure, she didn't have a 9–5 or the eldercare responsibilities she sustained for so long, but she was still a full-time, homeschooling mom of her special needs child and a present, active mother for her four older children—one with Type 1 diabetes. All of that was layered with the genuine burnout of brain and body she was facing thanks to several really intense years. It was no wonder that what used to be easy for Tonia now felt so laborious—she simply didn't have the same amount of energy as before, and through no fault of her own.

With that validation in hand, we decided to design an "art time" habit that would be flexible enough to better match the unexpected, constant, and urgent demands she experienced. It also accounted for a spectrum of good to bad energy days. As Tonia implemented and stuck to this habit, she was not only thrilled to have a habit that helped her feel like herself again, but also for the first time in a long while she could see herself as diligent, capable, and good at follow-through.

While there's some conflicting research on willpower (Is it a bank that gets depleted or can it be replenished throughout a single day? The answer is yes to both!),[5] energy expended throughout a woman's day is more urgent in nature, and also at a higher frequency than her male counterparts. This is why women "give up" when it takes 2.5 hours to do 14 minutes of their 20-minute workout. Their energy has gone to too many other responsibilities,

---

[5] Nir Eyal, *Indistractable: How to Control Your Attention and Choose Your Life* (BenBella Books, 2019).

with little hope of replenishing the willpower bank—a restoration that ironically often requires energy to build back up. And yet, instead of rightfully pointing to invisible labor as the culprit, many women, like Tonia, blame themselves for their supposed lack of willpower.

GMGMs Are Too Reliant on Predictability

After starting some light childcare for my four-month old baby, I finally had a more reliable schedule. Three days a week, my sitter would tend to the baby for three hours, and I would settle in to catch up on a month's worth of work. One day early on with this new schedule, I arrived at my desk, plopped down in my chair, and turned on my computer—excited for this new dependability of a few dedicated work hours I could now count on each week. About 30 minutes in, I saw a text from my neighbor, Deborah, "Monica, can you come help me?" Deborah was an elderly deaf woman whom we had done our best to form a friendship with, encouraging her to let us know whenever she needed something.

I walked over right away and discovered that Deborah was trying to communicate with a serviceman over some rat problems she had been having, but it wasn't going well. I did my best to relay the information from my neighbor to the worker, pointing out the areas she and I had already gone over a few days prior, and ensuring she understood what he thought they should do, and at what cost. With all the repeating and writing and communicating to be done, the time slipped by. Once I finally sat back down in my office chair, I had just 30 minutes left to scramble and complete my work.

So much of invisible labor is relationship-driven, and people are as unpredictable as their needs. We can have all of the plans in the world, but plans go up in smoke when your daughter accidentally leaves her lunch at home and knows she's not supposed to get school lunch, or when an elderly neighbor needs assistance, or a boss asks you to get snacks for the work party this afternoon.

I had the privilege of coaching a 72-year-old woman, and even then her biggest obstacle to forming consistent habits for herself was lack of predictability. She often needed (and chose) to be available at a moment's notice for her five adult children and many grandchildren. When she said, "My days are just so packed, and I never quite know how they'll pan out," I felt that sort of pang you do when you realize that some problems you face now will *always* be problems.

Habit bro methods don't have that kind of unpredictability in mind, nor do they view willpower as a finite resource, or at least one that varies from person to person.

I can illustrate this in one very important way, and—much like Eve Rodsky—by asking you a simple question: ***"How long does it take to form a habit?"***

I have asked this question of hundreds of women over several years. I have *never* gotten an answer outside of these numbers: 21 days, 28 days, 30 days, 100 days, and (very rarely shared) 1,000 days.

Where do these numbers come from? Good Men and their Great Methods. We all simply *know* the number of days we need to do a habit in order for it to stick. But, regardless of which number you volunteer, it's dependent on one thing: consistency.

You do the same habit, in the same way, at the same time of day, day after day until you meet the number required and now you officially have a habit. Simple, right? In theory, yes. For most women's reality, no.

And yet, instead of faulting these unrealistic numbers and standards, women blame themselves.

Habits do in fact live and die by consistency, just not in the way we've been taught. And habits do still require a level of repetition that eventually leads to unconscious behavior, but also not in the way we've been taught. I will soon teach you both with the Sticky Habit Method.

It's Time to Do Habits Differently

Wow—what a depressing book so far! If the odds are really that stacked up against us, is there any hope? Should we just give up now?

No, because we are *women*. We are strong, we are dependable, and we show up. We show up for our jobs, we show up for our babies, we show up to stock the right mustards, we show up to fold the towels, we show up to help our neighbors, we show up to clean the dang toilet.

We just need to do habits differently.

While there is a great deal of work to be done the world over on how we view women, support them, value them, and distribute the loads they carry, that is the kind of work that requires a great deal of time, not to mention shifts in culture, society, and even policy. It is necessary work, and one I personally strive to contribute to.

But, women need help now. This is why women deserve supportive habits, not just so they can show up as themselves to meet their responsibilities, but because they are human and deserve to value themselves as a priority, too.

This is where the Sticky Habit Method comes in as *the* guide for women to form habits that stick. These are the kinds of habits that help women reclaim their lives, feel supported, and able to consistently show up as themselves.

TAKEAWAYS: Popular habit formation methods weren't designed with women in mind. Thanks to invisible labor, women experience more interruptions, require more flexibility, lack predictable circumstances, and have less time, energy, and support. Habit bro methods often don't translate to women's lives because they're too reliant on willpower and too reliant on predictability. Women must do habits differently.

TAKE THOUGHT: How have you blamed yourself for your habit failures? How does validating your unique habit obstacles as a woman free you up to do habits differently?

TAKE ACTION: Track how many times you get interrupted for a period of time (morning, afternoon, or night).

NOTE: For more (printables, recommended books, complementary podcast episodes, etc.), remember to check out the free and included Sticky Habit resources, available online at https://stickyhabitsbook.com/resources:

Part Two

REDEFINE: WHAT HABITS ARE AND HOW THEY ARE FORMED

Habit Story 1

Name: Amanda

Responsibilities: Stay-at-home mom to four young children

Habit fail: Exercise

Amanda didn't know how she had gotten to this place. Exercise used to be something she did without much thought—a true habit. But now, it was like asking for the world each day to make time for a 30- to 60-minute workout. Why? It was more like "how?" Between the only affordable gym being quite far away and a toddler who didn't like childcare at the gym, Amanda had to fit her exercise into the cracks of her day. But those cracks were never dependable, as they hinged on her husband's availability to watch the children—and with him working 30–45 minutes away due to traffic, she never knew exactly when he was coming or going. When he was home, she had to choose between workouts at the gym and family responsibilities. The only other alternative was to work out early in the morning, but Amanda was in a season of needing to prioritize sleep as her toddler was not doing well in that department.

Exercise came at such a high cost. Amanda was both confused and angered by her own "ineptness" at getting it done when it used to be so easy in her past life.

Alongside Amanda, take one of your own "habit fails" (a habit you failed at) and apply what you are about to learn to help you understand why the failure wasn't *you*: it was your method.

We will begin by redefining what habits are and how we *think* they're supposed to be formed.

Chapter 4

Change the Way You See and Create Habits

Learn: The four habit types (Habiteers), their pitfalls to forming sustainable habits, and four habit maxims that fix those weaknesses

When you hear the word *habits*, what do you think of? Here are some answers I've received over the years:

- Things I'm supposed to do
- Automatic behaviors
- Expectations I can't meet
- Necessary duties
- Pressures to be someone I'm not
- Prescriptions
- Ways I "should" be living
- Balls and chains

Habits go deeper. The way you view habits affects the way you attempt to form and to maintain them. To truly change the way you do habits, you have to start by changing the way you *see* them.

To assist in this, I want to introduce you to some habit types.

What's Your (Habit) Type?

Growing up in the 1990s, I was quite aware of the Disney channel and the goings on there, despite not having cable television. I even knew of the famous Mouseketeers from *The Mickey Mouse Club*. This was a variety show that featured singing, dancing, and life lessons from young stars like Britney Spears, Justin Timberlake, Christina Aguilera, Ryan Gosling, and Keri Russell—all now big names who took up the honor of being young Mouseketeers. Each Mouseketeer had a sort of type: the brainy one, the funny one, the sporty one, the oddball . . .

Likewise, I want you to consider habits types—Habiteers, if you will—and how they interplay with the way we both see and create habits.

Each Habiteer carries preexisting ideals that act as pitfalls to creating sustainable habits. I want you to do away with these weaknesses. Instead of floating away into the ether, I will guide you to then replace that Habiteer's shoulds with my suggested habit maxims that come from the Sticky Habit Method, ones that fix these common pitfalls that show up in how women both define and form habits.

***The Martyr* believes that habits are balls and chains, aka "shoulds."**
Fix: Habits are *supportive*.

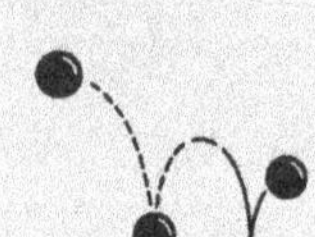

***The Dropper* believes that habits are routines.**
Fix: Habits are *small*.

***The Overachiever* believes you form habits through a "shoot-for-the-stars" strategy.**
Fix: Habits are *simple.*

***The Dangler* believes that habits should magically be inserted without much specificity**
Fix: Habits are *specific.*

To see which Habiteers you are prone toward, check out the 1990s-style personality quiz in the included online Sticky Habit resources, found at https://stickyhabitsbook.com/resources.

Habiteers That Define Habits

I'll now break down the weaknesses housed under each habit type, and what you can do to fix them. We'll start with Habiteers that *define* what habits are.

***The Martyr* believes that habits are balls and chains, aka "shoulds."**

What "shoulds" do you attach to exercise? (As a habits and identity coach, I've found that working out is the most common habit women want to gain.)

To count exercise as a habit, you likely believe you have to work out a minimum of 3 days a week, 30 minutes at a time, with a mix of cardio and strength training. This is a standard most of us learned while growing up, likely from a typical health class at school.

But for many women, that is just the start. A lot of us carry exercise standards that go well beyond that old school minimum. I've had women tell me that in order for exercise to count, they have to work out six days a week, with one hour devoted to cardio and one hour to strength training.

Similarly, think about any habit you'd like to work on: journaling, meditating, day planning, getting ready, meal prepping, and so on. Regardless of the habit, if you automatically pull up a well-defined prescription or a metric that you *have* to meet to be a good person or to count as someone with that habit, then you're likely a Martyr Habiteer.

Shoulds are one feature of this habit type, but another is feeling trapped. If your habits act more as prisons—that you are bound by them, that they demand exactness from you, and that there is no wiggle room—then it's no wonder you are resistant to forming habits.

Instead, look at habits as nets—ones that lift you up, allow some bend and flexibility, but are sturdy enough to catch you when you fall. Take the Martyr's view of habits, and replace the pressure-laced shoulds with this simple, but powerful one: **habits are supportive.**

Habits are there to support *you*, not the other way around. Put differently: habits should help, not hurt.

Believing that *habits are helpers* shifts the purpose habits serve in your life *and* the way they're allowed to look, too. You can do them in *your* way, and to match *your* season—not to meet some nebulous prescriptions performed with exactness.

This shift creates the flexibility you need to do the same habit but in a different way, depending on your season. And it's the first shift Amanda made that helped her fix her exercise problem.

AMANDA

"Okay, so if habits are 'supportive,' then I would actually consider working out from home. When exercise was a habit for me in the past, it was always at the gym. I can see now that I don't have to be there for it to count. I can still get a good workout in from home even without using weights, fancy equipment, or joining classes. And exercising from home would allow me to work out during naptime as well. I honestly haven't considered that as a possibility before!"

When habits are balls and chains, you become a Martyr imprisoned by them. You can't see all the options, you don't allow for seasonal flexibility, you become subservient to the standards you have been given or ones you were able to easily meet in the past.

Instead, owning that habits are helpers frees you up to see new possibilities and to be the designer of your own ideal habits—ones that match your personality, your preferences, and your season of life. (More on that later.)

I've seen this shift alone create dramatic transformations for women, both deep and practical. This is why before I teach you a single strategy, we start here: with changing the way you see habits.

Begin with this fundamental belief: ***habits are supportive.***

Let's turn to the next Habiteer.

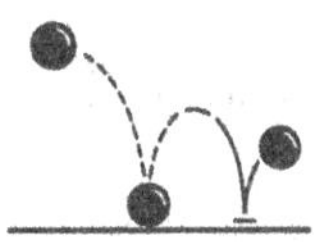

The Dropper **believes that habits are routines.**

Second to exercise, women most commonly want to improve how their mornings flow. When they state that desire, I usually ask them what an ideal morning would look like for them. They then rattle off a series of steps, like the following:

- Wake up before my family.
- Stretch and get on my workout clothes.
- Meditate.
- Prep breakfast and lunches for my kids.
- Take the kids to school.
- Go to the gym and exercise.
- Come home, shower, and get ready.

And they usually end that series with something like, "That's all!" like it really wasn't that much and they're a sloth for not being able to regularly do this "habit" yet.

What they're missing is that they aren't trying to install a habit, they're installing a *routine.* And routines require willpower—or like you learned, energy. Installing a full routine at once is like cashing out on an entire bank of energy at once. With this approach, you pay more in the long run, whether that price is more exhaustion, flaking out on other priorities, or dropping the "habit" altogether. This is how people take on the Dropper habit type.

You may think *routine* and *habit* are synonymous. They're not. **A habit is not a routine, but a routine can become habit.**

I usually get blank looks when I say this, so let me break it down another way.

Routines are a series of habits stacked together during a certain time frame and/or to meet a general purpose.

Think: morning routine, exercise routine, skincare routine, bedtime routine, meal prep routine, and so on.

It's not that you shouldn't want a routine—you absolutely can and should. It's that if you want a routine to run like a habit (meaning, it doesn't require tremendous effort), you have to acknowledge that the entire routine is actually made up of multiple habits.

To get that routine to stick, you instead choose to do habits differently by expending smaller amounts of energy as you build up a habit or two at a time. This enables you to work up to the ideal routine, and in ways that are far more sustainable and cost less of your energy bank over time. (Don't worry, I'll teach you more about this in Chapter 10.)

To combat the dropper mentality, own this maxim instead: **habits are small.**

In other words, one step from a fuller routine.

AMANDA

"The thing I'm struggling with about working out from home is this mindset that exercise is 'best' in the morning, and that I can't get ready until I've worked out. I feel the resistance of doing it any other time separate from a larger early morning routine. But with my toddler still waking up during the night, I know I need to prioritize my sleep. If I consider exercise as its own habit and allow it to match my season, then that again puts naptime on the table. It doesn't have to

be about me having an ideal morning—I just need to move my body and get those endorphins, even if it's midday, even if I already got ready earlier."

Thanks to owning that habits are small, Amanda was able to extract exercise from a prescribed, multi-stepped morning routine and move this singular habit to a time of day that worked better for her.

Owning that habits are small defies the toxic positivity sayings floating around in our heads:

"Today is the first day of the rest of your life!"
"Only *you* have the power to change your life."
"Don't settle for anything less than what you want!"

These platitudes pressure us to believe that the only way to make changes is via pure grit, to stay motivated, and exert self-discipline perfectly. We're similarly misled to install the ideal habit/routine with exactness starting day 1, moving through to at least day 21, and keeping the same habit for, well, the rest of our lives.

But, the people shouting these sayings at you are missing the energy—physical, mental, and emotional—that this method requires. They miss that pursuing all from all-or-nothing comes at a cost, whether that is a significant hit to your energy bank or you yelling more at your kids.

What prices have you paid in the past while forming habits in the all-or-nothing way? Can you consider what you have to gain by starting small instead? And what would change for you if you believed in the process to true and lasting growth: small wins build over time?

I know it's weirdly scary to believe, and I know it's intimidating to do habits differently. You do have an alternative—but the question is, does it actually work?

Some hope for those who are resistant or scared to start small: evidence from science and history shows us that small shifts create the biggest, most sustainable change. The compound effect is one such piece of evidence. Think of saving money: how a dollar a day saved is better than a lump of $20 each month, how investing takes those small amounts and, over time, grows the money to far larger sums. Small gains over time add up to big gains.

Believe that prioritizing small habits matters. Believe that they will grow, both in depth and in breadth. Believe that this is what sustainable habit formation looks like.

Habits are small.[1]

Our first two types of Habiteers lead us to redefine what habits are:

> **Habits are the *small* and *supportive* ways we consistently care for ourselves so that we can show up for ourselves and our responsibilities.**

Put simply: habits are the most basic form of self-care.

Habiteers That Define How Habits Are Formed

To fully redefine habits, we also need to redefine how they are formed. This is where the next two Habiteers enter the stage.

> ***The Overachiever* believes you form habits through a "shoot-for-the-stars" strategy.**

Even if you have the courage to start with *one* supportive habit, not a routine, you may still be falling apart at the implementation step if you begin with the ideal version of that habit.

---

[1] For those still worried, I also want to provide some hope: it *is* possible to form more than one habit at a time. More coming on that in an FAQ section after Chapter 11.

Confused? It's okay. We all have been, thanks to the "January Joiner" phenomenon when people save up their new habits for the New Year and then hit them hard. Such as, "Come the New Year, I will do the following":

- Go on a 30-minute walk every day.
- Do one guided meditation per evening.
- Plan out all meals for the week each Sunday.
- Journal a page a day.

Any to all of these habits sound small enough, except if you don't do any version of them yet, you're starting with the ideal—and ideals require energy. That's why you can either fizzle out doing the habits consistently, or yell at your kids more because, quite frankly, you're worn out.

Remember *all* comes at a cost, and those costs are most often our relationships, with others and with ourselves.[2]

Instead of believing that you have to start with *the* ideal version of the habit you want right away, embrace this new standard: **habits are simple.**

In other words, *start with the smallest and simplest version of your ideal.* I call this *the baseline.*

Baseline habit: the smallest and simplest version of an ideal habit.

Your baseline needs to be so small, you may be worried if it counts. It's the version of your ideal habit that you can do on a less-than-ideal kind of day, like when you're extra tired, when you or someone in your home is sick, when you have less time than normal, when the dog throws up on the couch . . . you get the picture.

[2]There are some habits you can't really inch your way up to, like when your family has to leave at an earlier time to make it to school on time after a summer of no alarms. Allow for those times and seasons, and in doing so give yourself the grace you (and others) need by acknowledging that you're paying a price that must be met. I'll talk more on this later.

Here are baseline versions of the ideal habits I introduced a moment ago:

- Go on a simple 30-minute walk every day → Go on a walk around the block.
- Do one guided meditation per evening → Take five deep breaths.
- Plan out all meals for the week each Sunday → Plan out easy dinners for three nights a week.
- Journal a page a day → Journal for one line.

I first learned of a concept similar to baselines from Stephen Guise's book, *How to Be an Imperfectionist.*[3] In it, he teaches about how ideals act like ceilings, the tippy-top of where we want to reach. But, to get there we also need floors, smaller versions of our ideals that act as the necessary foundation to help us better reach our desired ceilings.

For those who are uncertain if baselines are good enough, we are going to talk much more about them, but I want you to know this for now: ideals still matter. In fact, you'll see that casting a vision of your ideal habit is indeed part of the Sticky Habit Method. You *do* need to know where you're headed. But to get there both faster (trust!) and more sustainably (also, trust!), you need a baseline to act as the foundation to better meet that ideal with time.

AMANDA

"*Now that I'm owning that my workout doesn't have to be part of a bigger morning routine, I'm seeing that I still have it in my head that it needs to take at least an hour and cover both cardio and strength training. While I feel like I'm capable of doing that some days even now, if I were to simplify that to the baseline version for other days, I could choose cardio*

[3] Stephen Guise, *How to Be an Imperfectionist: The New Way to Self-Acceptance, Fearless Living, and Freedom from Perfectionism* (Selective Entertainment LLC, 2021).

or *strength training. Even 20 minutes*[4] *of either would still be a good workout, and I believe I could do that on my worst day. Heck, I could even do strength training without changing my clothes, since I'm doing a more gentle version of it! I already feel like this is going to happen."*

This is a good time to introduce my redefinition of consistency, one that pushes back on the habit bro version of consistency we have used as the standard forever:

Consistency is doing your best, most of the time, over time.

Your "best" doesn't equate to perfection; it's allowed to change—season to season and day to day. A baseline is your "best" on certain days and for certain seasons. (Little League baseball season, I'm looking at you.)

Your target for consistency is *more times than not.* What matters is doing a form of the habit more times than not, and over time.

This redefinition challenges the idea that flexibility and consistency are competing values. In truth, they are *complementary.* **Flexibility is what makes consistency possible.** Baselines act as the built-in flexibility that creates consistent habits, ones that make ideals more possible. Again, I'll teach more in depth on baselines soon—but for now, take on this belief:

Habits are simple.

There is one more habit type that spells disaster with traditional habit implementation.

[4] It's good to note that for many women, 20 minutes would be the ideal. Among other things, I want you to own that habits are subjective. Only *you* can know what is ideal and what is baseline for you. Since Amanda already had the habit of exercise for years before she hit roadblocks, we both felt confident that a 20-minute baseline would be doable for her. But for other women, five minutes would be better if they have never had the habit of working out consistently in the past. **Habits are subjective.**

***The Dangler* believes that habits should magically be inserted without much specificity.**

Going back to the January Joiner mentality, many of us think that to begin a new habit we simply decide a magical starting date and that's that.

Imagine a spider web. In order for it to be strong, it has to be attached to things; otherwise, it's dangly and will drift away. Habits—even if they're supportive, small, and simple—are dangling if they're not attached to other specifics. Already-existing habits are those specifics. This is often referred to as "habit stacking," and it's so much more than just piling on habits; it's about ensuring new habits stick.

Here are few examples of dangling habits, ones that still match the other "good habit shoulds" (supportive, small, and simple) we have walked through, but aren't *specific* enough to stick around:

- I will walk around the block in the mornings.
- I will journal for one line before bed.
- I will write down my three most important to-dos each day.
- I will take five deep breaths before I start my day.
- I will read for 15 minutes each afternoon.

Each of these habits are baselines—good! But, even while the women setting out to make them have designed a supportive, small, and simple habit to act as the baseline to their ideals, they are each lacking the *specifics* that create the strength they need to stay—bad!

Habits are specific.

Unattached habits are unsticky habits; attached habits are sticky habits.

To rectify these plans, you need to get super specific. We do this by defining the time of day, then deciding which *existing* habit the new one can be attached to. Did you see the key word there? ***Existing.*** I call this a *When-Then Pairing*. It's habit stacking, but nailed down to specific *timing*.

(NOTE: When I reference individual steps from the When-Then Pairing, each step will be capitalized and italicized.)

WHEN = existing habit

THEN = new habit

Example: *WHEN* I start the dishwasher, *THEN* I'll go wash my face.

To be successful with a new habit, you must attach it to one that already takes place during that time you'd like to have the new one. And this is where I am sure you'll throw up your hands because "Monica! I'm here to learn about habits because I don't have any!!!"

Yes, yes you do. You just don't realize it because they're already . . . (wait for it) . . . habits.

Let's take one of the earlier dangling habit examples and I'll walk you through the process to come up with a When-Then Pairing.

Dangling habit: I will walk around the block in the mornings.

The good news here is that this woman has decided on a time of day. That's the first step! With that timing in mind, I'd ask her what typically happens in the mornings. She may say things like "I wake up a little before the kids and get dressed, then help them get ready for school, I make them breakfast, they make their lunches, I wipe off the counter, I take them to school, I come home, I load the dishwasher and clean up breakfast, then I shower and officially get ready for the day."

Once she has a good list of the usual happenings, then I'd ask her, "Ideally within those usual tasks, *when* would you like to walk?" That answer would help us identify the gap in her already existing habits that we could insert the new walking habit into. Let's imagine this woman says, "It would be best for me to walk after dropping off the kids and before I clean up the kitchen. Otherwise, I get going cleaning or doing other home tasks and the morning slips away."

With that timing established, then I would help her decide which already-existing habit makes the most sense. "I guess when I drop off the kids, I can see I have the habits of turning off the car, closing the garage, and hanging up my keys. I think the last one would be a good *WHEN* habit to start with."

So, now we have her When-Then Pairing, and with that an **attached habit: *WHEN* I hang up my keys, *THEN* I will go directly outside for my walk.**

There is more to this—I would advise this woman to get on her workout clothes when she gets dressed in that morning rush, and there's actually a third step after the When-Then Pairing (more on that later!), but this habit stacking creates the foundation to forming an attached habit, because it is now so specific.

AMANDA

Amanda and I walked through a similar process when coming up with her own When-Then Pairing. Mind you, this was after we lowered some hurdles, such as ensuring she knows where she will exercise (in the family room) and that she has an easy setup there (weights, bands, and a mat on the side of the couch). Here's how it went for her.

"I feel so good about knowing both where I'm headed with my ideal and where I'm starting with my baseline. When I think about exercising during naptime, I know I have to start as soon as I am done putting my toddler down; I don't want to talk myself out of it or get distracted by another to-do. I always sing her a song while rocking her, then turn on her sound machine, turn off the light, put her down in the crib, and sneak out, closing the door behind me. I feel like closing the door could be my WHEN*! So,* WHEN *I close the door,* THEN *I'll go right to the family room and pick up my weights. That's it! On my worst day, I can do that and get my movement in for a minimum of 20 minutes."*

Habits are specific.

With the original two Habiteers (Martyr and Dropper) redefining habits, these two additional Habiteers (Overachiever and Dangler) have opened up the opportunity—necessity, even—to redefine how habits are formed.

Habits are formed by thoughtfully crafting a small, simple, and specific habit that supports our wants and needs, and then by consistently honoring that habit's baseline.

Here is a visual reminder of common habit pitfalls represented by Habiteers, and their fixes.

The Martyr **believes that habits are balls and chains, aka "shoulds."**
Fix: Habits are supportive.

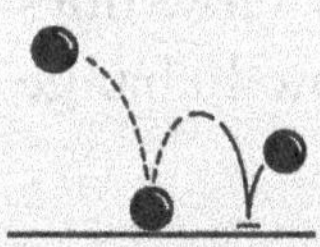

The Dropper **believes that habits are routines.**
Fix: Habits are small.

The Overachiever **believes you form habits through a "shoot-for-the-stars" strategy.**
Fix: Habits are simple.

The Dangler **believes that habits should magically be inserted without much specificity**
Fix: Habits are specific.

I don't want you to be a Martyr, Dropper, Overachiever, or Dangler anymore.[5] I want you to take on a whole new habit type, the Habiteer I call the ***Revolutionizer.***

[5] Remember, go to our free resources online to take the Habiteer Personality Quiz to find out which habit type you gravitate to the most. You can find that at https://stickyhabitsbook.com/resources.

TAKEAWAYS: Many of us carry preexisting ideals on what habits are and how they are formed. Habiteers (the Martyr, Dropper, Overachiever, and Dangler) are habit types that illustrate these ideas and their pitfalls: habits are shoulds, habits are routines, habits are formed by shooting for the stars, and habits are magically inserted without specificity. Instead, adopt habit maxims from the Sticky Habit Method that fix these weaknesses: habits are supportive, small, simple, and specific. The woman who owns these new ideals is a Revolutionizer.

TAKE THOUGHT: When you consider your own habit fail that you brought to mind at the beginning of Part Two, how did a Habiteer (or two) influence its demise? How does redefining what habits are and how they are formed change things for you personally?

TAKE ACTION: Take the Habiteer Personality Quiz (available as a printable) to see what habit pitfalls you tend to gravitate to.

NOTE: For more (printables, recommended books, complementary podcast episodes, etc.), remember to check out the free and included Sticky Habit resources, available online here:

Chapter 5

Become a Revolutionizer

Learn: What a Revolutionizer is, how to become one, and why you're still allowed to be you *as a Revolutionizer*

To see and do habits differently requires the courage of a revolutionizer: someone who is willing to do things that challenge the norms, to forge a new way, and all with a greater purpose in mind. This is who you need to be to do habits differently.

A Revolutionizer redefines habits and the habit formation process. They believe in and practice the Process. They learn from their failures. And they follow the Sticky Habit Method to form supportive habits that stick for the season they need them in.

You'll learn the official Sticky Habit Method (SHM) in Chapter 6. But first, I want to break down how the Revolutionizer (a good Habiteer!) redefines habits and the habit formation process.

As a reminder, we have already learned the following:

- **Habits are the *small* and *supportive* ways we consistently care for ourselves so that we can show up for ourselves and our responsibilities.**
- **Habits are formed by thoughtfully crafting a small, simple, and specific habit that supports our wants and needs, and then by consistently honoring that habit's baseline.**

But do you actually believe this yet?? Doing so requires you to change, starting with challenging the beliefs you've long stockpiled without even being cognizant of doing so. It also demands that you believe in a new way, and that might be the scariest step of all—to let go of the fallacy of "overnight success" and to instead own the true process for sustainable change: **small wins build over time.**

In her book *The Small and the Mighty*,[1] "America's government teacher," Sharon McMahon, talks about the "small" figures who made a huge difference over time in historical revolutions, from the Suffrage Movement to the Civil Rights Movement. As a guest on my podcast, Sharon remarked on what these historical revolutionizers exemplified:

> *Almost all of the important change that has happened in the grand sweep of history has come incrementally. The power of incremental change is undeniable . . . . Civil Rights was the product of 70 years plus of hard work. Most important lasting change . . . comes with incremental progress, the result of long years of hard work.*

True revolutionizers (from history to habits) believe in small wins building over time.

---

[1] Sharon McMahon, *The Small and the Mighty: Twelve Unsung Americans Who Changed the Course of History, From the Founding to the Civil Rights Movement* (Thesis, 2024).

The Process

I have referenced this principle so often over the years that I have called it *the Process*. This truth pairs nicely with what you'll learn with the SHM, but it also transcends habits—it's about any kind of progress you desire to make.

The Process: small wins build over time.

I once hosted a group coaching program and guided about 20 women through the Process to overcome how their perfectionist tendencies were blocking their progress. Early on, a woman I'll call Julie took the hot seat and it was immediately clear that she was unconvinced. How could she change in the deepest, most important ways if she was no longer a perfectionist? Don't big shifts require big efforts?

The thing is, Julie did need to make some big changes, inside and out. But, her lifelong methods of doing so involved a tremendous amount of work propelled by a heavy dose of shame. (Perfectionists feed off of shame—much more on that in Chapter 11.) Looking back, Julie could only see one way of trying and doing.

In some ways, it had paid off for her. Julie had experienced some major accomplishments in her life. But, if she was being honest with herself, Julie could now acknowledge that those achievements came at a cost—her mental health being one and not being able to sustain her growth being another. Because she was tired of failing, she desired a new way to create needed change. But, it was terrifying to make that leap.

I challenged Julie to simply *try* another way: to make room for the mess of being human, to build one small win at a time, to persist in a new way—not with urgency and pressure, but with belief and patience. Julie was still not fully convinced of the Process, and she even felt a little scared. And yet, she was willing to try.

At the end of the program, we all gathered in our online Zoom session and Julie took the hot seat again. We celebrated the progress she had made on her way to bigger change, and even more importantly how this growth was done in ways that required small, steady, and compassionate steps. Julie was doing it! And she was beginning to reap the benefits, too. It was then that Julie took a trembling breath and said something I have never, ever forgotten: **"I've learned it takes the greatest of courage to do the smallest of things."**

The silence on the other end of that statement was loud. We all heard it, and we all felt it. I saw little squares of other program participants nodding their heads, some visibly crying. Julie was right. It takes the greatest of courage to do the smallest of things.

To be a Revolutionizer, you must have that courage. You must believe in *and* practice the Process. This means you have to also have the courage to fail.

An Important Note on Failure

Another coaching client from that same program bemoaned, "I don't like to learn from failure."

My response to her was, "Then you don't like to learn."

The most successful people in the world understand the truth about failure: it's not personal. They know that *everyone* experiences failure on the path to progress. When they fail (not *if*, when!), they get curious instead of judgmental. They practice the growth mindset, knowing that the way they perceive problems alters the way they show up to them.

Carol Dweck, an American psychologist and academic at Stanford University, has long studied the growth mindset and its opposite, the fixed mindset. She writes, "In the fixed mindset, everything is about the outcome. If you fail—or if you're not the best—it's all been wasted. The growth mindset allows people to value what they're doing regardless of the outcome."[2]

---

[2] Carol Dweck, *Mindset: The New Psychology of Success* (Random House, 2006).

In other words, Dweck's research supports something I've long anecdotally experienced and taught—***the transformation lies in the process, not the outcome.***

Failure is not fun.

I'm the first to say it. I don't enjoy failing, and I don't actively seek it out. However, making space for failure has been one of the most vital ways (if not *the* most) I've been able to stay on the path to progress. (You never fully "arrive," by the way.)

When you adopt the growth mindset, you can own that failure doesn't mean you're doing it wrong—it means you're doing it right.

I like to think about progress as a vehicle on the highway. As you drive, you will often drift from one side of your lane to the other, requiring constant mini-adjustments to ensure you're headed where you need to go. At times, you may cross lanes, get off at the wrong exit, take side roads and dirt roads, or even have to stop along the way to recoup, refuel, or make repairs. But as long as you do your best to be pointed in the right direction, then you are doing it right.

The same Civil Rights revolutionizers that McMahon referenced endured 70+ years with less-than-ideal results. They didn't expect change to entail smooth sailing, and that expectation enabled them to persist. They knew they were doing things right because they were doing what they could.

When you similarly embrace that the path to progress involves failure, you won't jump right off when it happens. Instead, you'll expect missteps, engage with frustrations differently, and keep riding the ups and downs any worthy venture brings.

Habit fails will be no different. Revolutionizer Habiteers understand this. When their habits fail, instead of blaming themselves they blame the habit plan. They insert compassion and objectively analyze what happened. They forge ahead with information instead of shame. Revolutionizers don't let a missed day (or several) stop them from learning and trying again. They embody a gentler, but still diligent, form of persistence.

You Can Still Be You as a Revolutionizer

Being a Revolutionizer doesn't mean you look like all the others. It means you look (and feel!) like yourself. There is no single type of "habit person." Once you fully own the mindset shifts you've learned from Part Two (habits are supportive, small, simple, and specific), you will also own that you can be a habit person in a way that's right for *you*.

Another habit truth: **habits are subjective**.

What one person may deem as a "bad habit" may be a "good habit" for another (e.g., watching Netflix each night). What one person designs as a baseline may be an ideal for someone else (e.g., 20 minutes of exercise). And how one person defines what it looks like to be a "habit person" can oppose another's point of view.

Maybe you are naturally more regimented, or more go with the flow. Perhaps your season of life right now is so intense that your personal habits need to counterbalance all the stress. Or you are moving into a time with more room and more energy, so your habits can be stepped up a notch. Regardless, supportive habits are for every type of Revolutionizer. And every type of Revolutionizer is a "habit person."

AMANDA

"Monica, I can't believe this, but I have been exercising consistently!"

Amanda and I were checking in by email a few months after our coaching call. I could feel her newfound confidence radiating from my screen. I smiled as I read Amanda's message, "I'm so proud of myself. I've literally only missed like 2 days of working out! I always do at least 20 minutes. I can't believe I've stuck with it. I feel so, so good."

I was proud of Amanda, but I wasn't surprised—both by the habit but also how she felt about herself. Because of the mindset shifts she made, Amanda had the freedom to create a consistent habit that worked for her. In the process of redefining what habits are and how they are formed, Amanda also reshaped the way she saw herself. She was finally doing the thing she had long said she wanted to do: she was on her own list. And while 20 minutes a day wouldn't make her an Olympian, it didn't need to. Consistently exercising made Amanda feel stronger and more supported, inside and out. And that was far more than she had initially bargained for.

Like Amanda, are you ready to revolutionize the habit formation process? It's time to dive into learning (and applying!) the method Revolutionizers follow: the Sticky Habit Method.

Haven't heard of it? It's because it's my own process and it's new to you. The Sticky Habit Method was created because of everything you just read about failure and persistence. It's *the* method for busy women who have less time, low energy, and limited support, and are still deserving of habits that help them reclaim happiness in their lives.

Following this section, you'll see an overview of the Sticky Habit Method (which I'll mostly refer to as SHM). You don't need to memorize the overview of the method; you don't even need to understand it yet. But, it's a good page to bookmark so you can come back and reference where you're at in the SHM and what's coming up next.

Speaking of which, as you take on the Revolutionizer Habiteer and proceed through learning and applying the Sticky Habit Method, I'd encourage you to do so in real time, step-by-step. Why not try? And if you fail, I'll teach you what to do with that failure. You've got nothing to lose.

TAKEAWAYS: To view and do habits differently, you need to embody the Revolutionizer Habiteer. Revolutionizers redefine habits and the habit formation process. They believe in and practice the Process, that small wins build over time. They both expect and learn from their failures. And they follow the Sticky Habit Method to form supportive habits that stick for the season they need them in.

TAKE THOUGHT: How has your fear of failure held you back in the past? What is preventing you from seeing yourself as a habit person now, and how can you challenge those beliefs?

TAKE ACTION: Think about a failure you experienced. Ask yourself how a Revolutionizer would have moved through that, and how you can do so yourself as you move forward.

NOTE: For more (printables, recommended books, complementary podcast episodes, etc.), remember to check out the free and included Sticky Habit resources, available online at https://stickyhabitsbook.com/resources:

A Visual Breakdown of the Sticky Habit Method

Dog ear or bookmark this page to reference the Sticky Habit Method as you go and for any time you're wanting to form a new habit. If you don't understand something now, you will!

Part Three of this book will teach the first phase of the method, and Part Four will cover the rest.

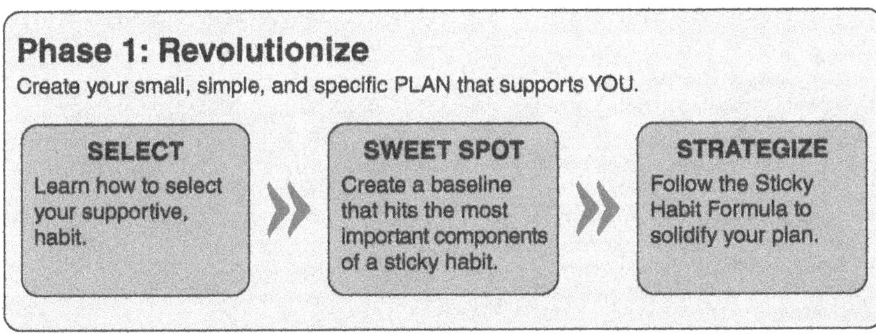

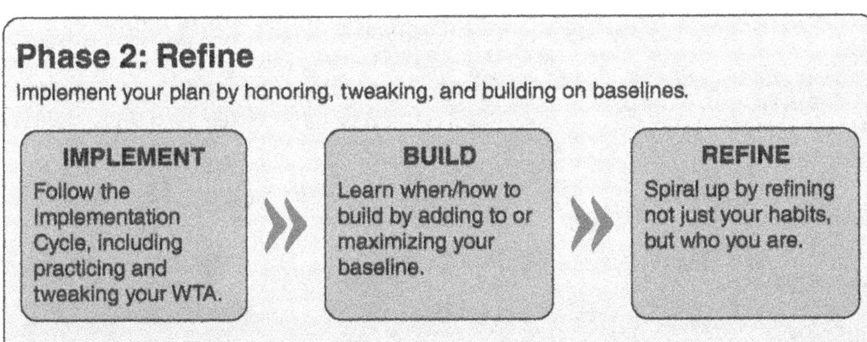

Part Three

REVOLUTIONIZE: PHASE ONE OF THE STICKY HABIT METHOD

Habit Story 2

Name: Patrice

Responsibilities: Working grandmother

Habit fail: Family history

Scrapbooking and filling the gaps in her family's genealogical tree were things Patrice had long loved to do—so why wasn't she? Patrice didn't trust herself. Over and over, she said she would prioritize habits, from family history to going to bed earlier, only to never do them. Now in her 60s, Patrice honestly wondered if it was too late for her, and not just to make habits. Thanks to decades of trying and failing, or stopping at the starting line, Patrice no longer believed herself when she set out with good intentions. She wondered if maybe she really was just an old dog and the days of learning new tricks were far behind her. And yet . . . Patrice knew in her heart that she wanted things to be different; she wanted to be *different. So maybe, just maybe, she could try again, but try in a new way.*

Now that we have redefined what habits are and how they are formed, it's time to learn phase one of the Sticky Habit Method: Revolutionize: create a small, simple, and specific plan that supports you. We begin by learning how to choose the habit you want to work on. This selection step is far more important than you may think.

Chapter 6

Select

Learn: The first pillar of the Sticky Habit Method: Select a supportive habit

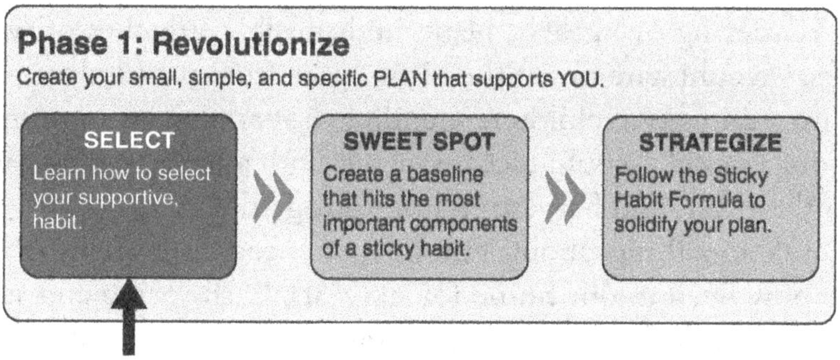

(Each chapter that teaches the Sticky Habit Method will include a mini-version of the method noting where we are so you can keep track.)

I never had a green thumb. While living in our little house in California, I would buy a basil or tomato plant, plop it next to the back door, and do my best to stay on top of watering it.

But for whatever reason, the plant would soon look sick and die. My tiny yard always overwhelmed me. I wanted it to look and function so differently, but my insecure efforts and lack of know-how gradually forced an acceptance that we were "crummy yard people." I had no confidence in my ability to grow green things and keep them that way.

Once we moved to Utah, we bought an old home with a big backyard that had been neglected for decades. Standing at the back of the house and looking out, the yard takes on a baseball diamond shape, getting wider the more it moves back with lots of space to play, explore, and possibly even grow things. With a bundle of active kids who do better with regular time outdoors, the backyard was the main reason we bought our house. Despite my extensive history with a black thumb, the new-to-me yard pushed me to think bigger than my past.

Ever the Anglophile, I envisioned our backyard as a wild English countryside space, with gravel pathways and many garden boxes bordering overgrown plants and possibly stretches of wildflowers. I would stare out at the blank space from my kitchen window, imagining our children spending hours and hours outside like I did as a kid. I could picture myself with a big straw hat tending to the plants and harvesting from our garden.

Here's the thing about visions: you need to execute them. We've now lived in our home for six years. Each spring and summer, we've worked to build the backyard of my British countryside dreams, adding one element here, and another there. The garden especially has involved a great deal of time and tutelage, from gradually installing each of the 16 garden boxes (I know!), to learning how to grow one plant at a time. Now, after several growing seasons of failing and learning, I tend to have a beautiful, blossoming garden.

With each passing harvest, I've grasped the seeds of my own potential. *I've learned that I am capable of change.* Once a plant murderer, now I have new evidence proving otherwise, and with it a rising challenge to all of my long-held self-doubts.

Habit Garden

When we are learning to form habits, we are much like I was while looking out the kitchen window of my home—we don't want just a habit here or there, we want a flourishing, interconnected network of habits. We want the full habit garden. But, just like gardening, if you want the full product, it's best to start by learning how to grow one, two, maybe three habits at first. Then, you can take what you learned and gradually build a habit garden of your dreams. Along the way, you'll challenge old patterns that formed old identities; you'll embrace the seeds of your true potential.

As we learned with the Dropper and Overachiever Habiteers, one of the reasons why you may have experienced habit fails in the past is that you went for the proverbial full garden instead of the single plant or garden bed. I want to encourage you to first learn and apply (!) the Sticky Habit Method (SHM) with a single habit, not because you aren't capable, but because this is a new skill set and unlike anything you've done or tried with habits before. Once you've learned to grow a single habit that sticks, you can grow many more—a lifetime amount, really—and also eventually work on a few habits at once.

Sticky Habit Elements

The first step of the SHM is *Select.*

Both now and later, selecting the habit you want to work on is pivotal. Just like soil needs certain elements for seeds to grow and to thrive (nitrogen, phosphorus, potassium, etc.), your chosen habit needs certain components to set up its success. Ensuring your habit has some to many of these elements will make your habit supportive and more likely to truly stick.

Sticky Habit Elements

Components that help make habits sticky:

Keystone	**Feel-Good**
Seasonal	**Controllable**
Desirable	**Feelings Focused**

Keystone

Have you ever seen an old stone archway? The most important stone of the lot is at the very top. It's the stone that is holding up all the others: the keystone. Similarly, the habit(s) you choose to work on should carry that level of importance.[1] (It's possible to have more than one keystone habit, but I recommend working on just one at a time.)

Back when my podcast, *About Progress*, was shifting from a hobby into a business, I hired my first business coach. His group coaching program was $300 a month, a massive expense for me since I wasn't making any money from my show and we were already on a very tight budget at home. You better believe that I moved heaven and earth to attend every single weekly session, furiously writing page after page of extensive notes. I was *ready* and willing to turn my passion into a thriving business.

In one of these sessions, I got to be in the hot seat and get coached one-on-one. My coach and I went through the big dreams I had for my new business, defining these dreams into goals for the here and now. It was then that my coach asked me, "Monica, what is the *one* thing that will make all of these goals more possible?"

I knew immediately, and sheepishly responded, "Sleep."

[1] Charles Duhigg's book, *The Power of Habit: Why We Do What We Do in Life and Business* (Random House, 2014), has a great section on keystone habits.

If I actually slept better, I would have the energy and the (day) time to put the right kind of effort into my newly claimed business. Fascinatingly, out of all the things on my list full of ways I was ready to learn, work, and grow, sleep wasn't on there. And yet, it was the *very* thing that would make the entire list possible.

This was right around the "family pictures gone awry" time where my vanity pushed me to finally prioritize my own personal habits, sleep being paramount. With these two experiences happening back-to-back, there was no question in my mind that sleep had to be my keystone habit.

What is one habit that would make everything else in your life more possible? When you start doing habits differently, I'd encourage you to consider choosing a keystone habit that would make the biggest difference for you and help shore up other habits' success, too.

If you're struggling to come up with a keystone, there are other ways to pick your habit. Keep reading!

Seasonal

Put simply, the habit(s) you work on should be applicable and practical for your season, and your season can be both literal (winter, spring, summer, fall) or figurative (phase of life).

This is where we have to take an honest account of what our season's limitations are and work *with* them, rather than against them. Sometimes, that means a habit needs to wait for a different time. Other times, it's the same habit but done in a different way.

When I was postpartum with my first three kids, I went right back into exercising as usual, running far sooner, harder, and farther than I had any business doing and typically while pushing a kid or two in our running stroller. Thanks to the havoc this wreaked on my pelvic floor, I had to dramatically change my lifestyle and sadly quit running on doctor's orders. Otherwise, I was told I'd need a hysterectomy and full reconstruction surgery. (Remember in Chapter 1 when I told you my only consistent habit as a young, self-sacrificial mom was a crazy amount of running? I told you I paid a price for it—this was it.)

Second to sleep, exercise is my most supportive habit. It helps me manage my anxiety and keep depressive episodes at bay or lessen their effects when they do come. Postpartum tends to be a *very* anxious time for me, so moving my body is crucial if I want to show up as the mom I want to be. In the past, I paid a dear price for neglecting to make my exercise habit seasonal, forcing the right habit but in the wrong way. So, I learned to make movement during my final two postpartum seasons both paramount and practical.

With my last baby, I started with my seasonal baseline of 10 minutes of gentle movement—stretching, yoga, light walks. Those 10 minutes weren't about losing my "baby weight" (Can we just stop with that?), they were about feeling like myself. And thanks to this standard, not only did I take the proper amount of time to heal but I still had the support I needed to work through what turned out to be a very challenging time in my life.

Not accounting for your season leads to habit fails. So, work with what you've got. Are you dealing with depression at the moment? Is it your kids' sports season? Or perhaps a busier time at work? Don't ignore what is happening in your life while designing a habit; instead, make your season an essential factor while you design a supportive habit that sticks.

Desirable

This may be the most overlooked element of a successful habit, especially because most people see habits as prisons. But, if you shift to viewing habits as helpers, that also means you know that you—yes, you—should actually *want* the habit(s) you choose to work on.

This is when I could say, "No shoulds allowed!" and "Stop 'shoulding' on yourself!" But, here's the thing—***shoulds can be chosen***.

You do need to be vigilant about not choosing habits just because you think you are supposed to have them. That's how we become Martyrs, right? However, it is possible to choose habits that otherwise easily could feel like prescriptions. In the *choosing*, you are allowed to design habits that match your wants, needs, preferences, and seasons.

Exercise is definitely the most should habit I've seen women carry around with them for their entire lives. If they *choose* this should (by owning it's a habit they do indeed *want*) that is when they are able to make their own prescription of a desirable form of working out. That has freed up many of my clients to lean into yoga, walking, hiking, dancing, and even stretching as exercise.

I've also seen countless women redefine what it looks like to journal, meditate, meal plan, and more. In redefining what counts, the habit feels more like something they actually *want*—in other words, desirable. Have you ever made desirability part of your habit selection process? It's a game changer.

Feel-Good

Hand in hand with desirable, habits can feel good!

We already discussed the importance of choosing the habit(s) you *want*, so how is feel-good different? It all comes down to brain science, something we are going to learn a surprising amount of.

Behaviors stick around—for good or for bad—because they create something that feels nice to the brain. You may recall the feel-good chemicals: dopamine, serotonin, endorphins, and oxytocin. Our ancient brains are designed to seek out these chemicals as a form of self-preservation and as a way to escape the stressors of life.

When what we do creates those chemicals, we instinctively seek out those behaviors over and over until they become habitual. This is true for "good" habits and for "bad."

Habits can be *just* about feeling good. Here are some of my favorites: watching a YouTube video while I eat my lunch, reading in the afternoons, learning how to sketch a flower on Sunday afternoons, sewing something fun after the kids are in bed.

And we can also design more productivity-based habits to feel good by pushing out those feel-good chemicals. That can happen by redefining what it looks like to make that habit "count," as referenced under the desirable element. But it can also happen with **pairing** (when we pair a blah! task with a yay! feeling, like listening to a book while washing the dishes) and **positive reinforcement** (when we create feel-good chemicals after completing a habit). Those are hacks I'll cover more in Chapter 8 and the FAQ section after Chapter 11.

Traditional habit bro methods are very reliant on willpower and self-discipline, like it's a character thing. While those aspects can be true to a certain extent, **habit formation is really a brain thing**.

To form habits that stick, we work *with* the brain, not against it, and we do so on multiple levels. From now on, you'll see a special brain hack stamp whenever what I teach serves as a way to *train your brain.*

Controllable

I know you are likely wanting to work on so many things, but don't fall for the trap of working on *all* the things, especially those that you can't reasonably control.

In my Heroic Coaching training, one of the most-used mantras was, "Control the controllables." This isn't about toxic positivity à la: "You must control everything through sheer grit." Instead, when you accept that it's best to control what is *truly* within your control, you recognize and accept your season's limitations and you don't seek to control others' behaviors, too. In other words: before you try to change your husband's habits, worry about your own first.[2]

With this element, I recommend selecting a habit that is all about *you* so that you have the best chance of success. What would help you feel more like yourself? What is a habit that would make life easier for you right now? What habit would act as a form of self-care for you and your season?

Selecting a habit that matches any of those questions is a surefire way to embody *control the controllables*. It also serves as a way for you to first learn the SHM before seeking to apply it to trickier habits, or ones that are more about being a productive member of society.

I always recommend that women think about what their most controllable time of day is. When are you least likely to be interrupted? When can you focus more on yourself instead of your responsibilities? For many women, that's the bookends of their day: the morning and the night. For others (especially those with teenagers in the home), it can be at other odd hours, like early afternoon.

You can better control the controllables by selecting a habit that is more within your own scope of controllability.

Feelings Focused

If all of these elements are helpful, but still not *quite* getting you across the habit selection finish line, here's one of my favorite ways to help women decide on a habit to work on:

1. Think about the general time of day you want to focus on the most (morning, after the kids are home from school, before bed, etc.).
2. Decide on how you want to *feel* during that time.
3. Brainstorm possible habits that would create that feeling.

---

[2] However, you can eventually transfer teachings from the SHM to help your kids learn to form habits that stick.

4. Select one that feels best aligned with some or all of the other elements discussed (keystone, seasonal, desirable, feel-good, and controllable).

Starting with the feelings may seem a little touchy-feely, but as women we have been judged for this disposition for millennia, so we might as well lean into something that is actually a strength.

If all else fails, start by focusing on the feelings.

Start with a Seed

You may not be able to hit every single element here, and you don't have to; but perhaps you'll be like Taryn from Chapter 3 and find *the* habit that checks off all the boxes. For her, that was Taryn Time, where Taryn would take a break after lunch to do something she always wanted to do but rarely found the time, like crafting or reading. This habit—a set aside time each day—acted as a key way for her to prioritize herself. Taryn *wanted* this ritual, she'd have flexibility to choose activities that felt good for her that day, it was at a time of day she could more easily control, and it would create the grounded feelings she really needed.

I know you want a flourishing habit garden, but will you start with one habit seed? To do so, I recommend beginning with a brainstorm of what habits you would potentially like, then filtering them through the elements you learned in this section. Here is a quick reference of them:

Sticky Habit Elements

Components that help make habits sticky:

Keystone	**Feel-Good**
Seasonal	**Controllable**
Desirable	**Feelings Focused**

To help with the brainstorming step, refer to the Sticky Habit Rainstorm. It's a printable where I rain down habit ideas onto your potential habit garden. You can find it in our included resources at https://stickyhabitsbook.com/resources.

Once you have selected the supportive habit you'd like to work on (both now and in the future), it's time to begin to design your habit implementation plan and, as part of that, what can make the habit doable, even on the worst of days.

PATRICE

Patrice already knew she wanted a habit that helped her lean into working on family history. So, what was getting in the way of her actually doing so? When we analyzed the habit itself, Patrice realized that she was operating on old prescriptions of both how she used to be able to do scrapbooking and family history, and how others had taught her to do so. In her current season of life, Patrice could not do that intensive of work as regularly as she wanted to. I asked Patrice how she'd like family history to feel, and she immediately responded, "connective." Patrice explained that even spending a little time in the past helps her feel more connected not only to the people she loves but also to herself and the present. Because of that, we were able to come up with more ideas on how that time could look if it were more regular and more desirable, ranging from organizing her scrapbooks, looking through them, extracting names from public records, writing stories of her loved ones, and more—all of which added to the connective feeling. Ultimately, Patrice decided that what was most controllable in her life right now was to have family history time set aside each day, and depending on how much time and energy she had to give, she could choose from that list of possible activities, all to connect with those from her past. Patrice made her own prescription.

TAKEAWAYS: The first step of the Sticky Habit Method is to ***select*** a habit to work on. Be sure that any to many of these elements are part of the habit you choose so it's extra sticky: keystone, seasonal, desirable, feel-good, controllable, and feelings focused. Habit formation is more of a brain thing. You'll learn more brain hacks to train your brain to form habits that stick.

TAKE THOUGHT: What habit would be very supportive for this season of your life? How do you want this habit to *feel*?

TAKE ACTION: Take a look at the Sticky Habit Rainstorm from the online resources for help selecting your habit.

NOTE: For more (printables, recommended books, complementary podcast episodes, etc.), remember to check out the free and included Sticky Habit resources, available online at https://stickyhabitsbook.com/resources:

Chapter 7

Sweet Spot

Learn: The second pillar of the Sticky Habit Method, the Sweet Spot, and how casting a vision and creating a baseline helps train your brain to form habits that stick

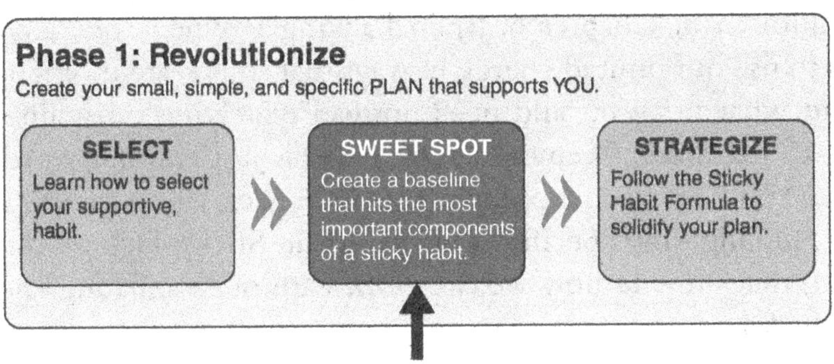

So much of our lives comes down to something I think we always *feel* but rarely validate: energy.

I'm talking physical, mental, spiritual energy. How much we have of it, how easily we can access it, and how regularly we can restore it truly affects every moment of every day. And yet, energy is something we almost never take into account for how we do life, including habits.

What if you don't have a discipline problem? What if you have an energy problem?

In my journey with sleep, I've learned that energy is not an endless resource inside of us. Rather, energy ebbs and flows depending on what we did that day, how well we slept the night before, how our mental faculties are doing, and how much outside support we get (not to mention our physical health!).

Nobody—and I mean nobody—can count on having the same amount of energy every single day. So, why do we pretend otherwise? (Cough . . . because we've been taught to.)

As Revolutionizers, we do habits differently. One of the most important ways we can do so is by honoring the ebbs and flows of our energy. To do that, we have to be more intuitive in ways that may feel foreign, but also life-giving. We have to work *with* our energy, limitations and all, instead of against it.

My number one way to do so is brain hacking, something I mentioned in Chapter 6. Brain hacking is when we train our brain to use our limited energy in ways that still create momentum toward what we want and need, instead of relying on willpower alone to get there. (Remember, *willpower* is just another word for *energy*.) You'll notice me pull out the brain hack stamp for the next while, highlighting specific tools from the Sticky Habit Method (SHM) that show us how we can work with our vacillating energy, in all its forms.

The Sweet Spot

After Select, the next step in the SHM is the *Sweet Spot*, when you begin to design your habit.

Just like any treasure hunter needs a map with an *X* that marks the spot, you need to know where you are headed with your habit. For us Revolutionizers, our map is the Sticky Habit Matrix, the center acting as its own *X*.

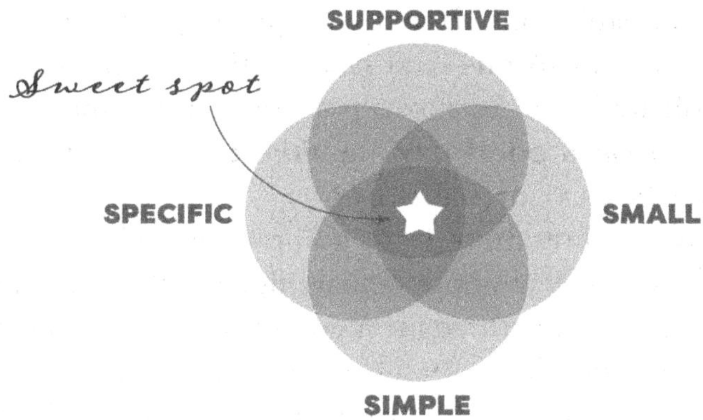

When you learned about the Habiteers, you also learned of the four maxims you need to consider to make a habit sticky. The habit should be supportive, small, simple, and specific. Each of these four maxims act as rings of the Sticky Habit Matrix. Right at the very center where they all meet is what I call the *Sweet Spot*, where a carefully designed habit will be best set up for success.

To find the Sweet Spot, do the following (note: the maxims are bolded):

1. Select a habit that feels **supportive** (you've done this!).
2. Cast a vision of your habit's ideal.
3. Form a baseline for your habit, one that is **small** and **simple.**
4. Strategize a **specific** habit plan.

The rest of this chapter will continue with steps two and three, and strategy will follow in the next chapter.

Cast a Vision

Stephen Covey was right about many things in his book *The 7 Habits of Highly Effective People*, but to me this may be the most important: begin with the end in mind.

Take the habit you selected—journaling, exercise, meditation, day planning, and so on—and cast a vision of that end. To assist (and to still push you to move past prescriptive shoulds), answer this question: **on a good day for *this* season, what would the ideal version of your habit be?**

By way of illustration, I am going to introduce you to Sally Down the Street, a symbolic female figure I'll use to apply what we are learning to the three most common habits women come to me wanting to develop: exercise, spiritual practice, and journaling.

Next, you'll see Sally, the habits she selected, and the ideal version of each habit.

Sally Down the Street: Ideals

EXERCISE: I will go for a three-mile walk around my neighborhood in the a.m., after my kids go to school.

SPIRITUAL PRACTICE: I will meditate 10 minutes in the early afternoon before the mad rush begins.

JOURNALING: I will write one page in my journal after I get ready for bed.

You can see that each of these ideals is designed with Sally in mind: What habit would feel good to her? How can even her ideal habit still reflect the nature of her current circumstances?

These ideals also embody two of the Sticky Habit Matrix's circles. You can see they are small (not a full routine) and supportive (reflective of her needs).

However, they are not the simplest version, nor specific enough . . . yet.

Ideals are *really* important. They define what matters to us, they help us envision what we are working toward, and they inspire us to get started. But, we often don't have ideal days or, as part of that, ideal amounts of energy we can rely on.

Here's where I have to say something that is true, but perhaps not what the Overachiever in you wants to hear:

> **Habits shouldn't be designed to be possible only on your best days; they should be designed to support you on your worst days.** BRAIN HACK

This is where baselines come in.

Form a Baseline

I've gently introduced you to baselines before, but now it's time to break them down deeply and practically, starting with a quick refresher:

> **A baseline is the smallest and simplest version of an ideal habit.**

A correctly designed baseline crosses off two needed maxims of the Sticky Habit Matrix: small and simple.

Taryn knew that in order to make Taryn Time sustainable, she had to be flexible with both the amount of time she allotted for herself and which activities she selected, all to match the fluctuating needs posed by her work and her energy levels. She decided her ideal amount would be 30 minutes to spend on an interest that sounded good that day, but her baseline would be five minutes of reading—both an amount of time and an activity so easy that she could do it on her worst day.

Remember, baselines need to be so small and so simple there is a part of you that wonders if they even count. But they do, and in multiple important ways, starting with the fact that baselines are the ultimate brain hack, tricking our brain into doing things even when we *really* don't feel like it. Here's how . . .

Baselines Make Consistency Possible-

It's true that habits live and die by consistency. Just not in the way we've been taught.

I would like you to revisit the definition of consistency I introduced to you in Chapter 4:

Consistency is doing your best, most of the time, over time.

This means a few things when it comes to baselines, specifically:

- Your best is allowed to change—season to season and even day to day.
- Your target for consistency is **more times than not**, not perfection. (Yes, hitting 4/7 days is consistent.)
- Your path to the ideal may seem to take longer and be more wandering, but sustainability is your destination.

If you truly want your ideal version of a habit instead of a momentary flash in the pan, you must once again believe that flexibility makes consistency possible. **Flexibility and consistency are not competing ideals—they are complementary**.

Baselines are the built-in flexibility we need to make habits consistent.

BRAIN HACK

Baselines create the flexibility we need to be consistent and, most importantly, to consistently have the support we deserve regardless of how ideal our days (and our energy) are. Baselines provide real support whether or not we are having a good day, whether or not we slept well, whether or not we get interrupted, whether or not we are on our periods. (Some examples of baselines are coming with Sally Down the Street!)

Baselines Create Momentum–

I am not known for my expertise in physics, but there are some things I learned from school that I could not forget if I tried.

It was weirdly a philosophy teacher in high school who illustrated so many principles of physics to our class, mostly by pitching a baseball at the metal wall of his portable classroom—an attention-grabbing move if there ever was one. That dumb baseball taught me about Einstein's laws of relativity and gravity, and Newton's laws of motion, among others. With the law of inertia, we learn that an object in motion stays in motion,[1] something made all the more apparent each time that ball loudly smacked the classroom's carpeted metal wall.

In a world where typical habit formation is so dependent on a superhuman level of motivation, I want you to *stop* waiting for that motivation, and instead do something to *start* creating momentum. This is what baselines do.

Baselines create momentum. BRAIN HACK

[1] The full law is "an object at rest stays at rest and an object in motion stays in motion with the same speed and in the same direction unless acted upon by an unbalanced force."

If it is not yet a habit, completing a full ideal version of the habit you would like requires a lot of energy. But, a baseline version of that same habit can get started with next to no energy. And when it gets going, the momentum often carries you to do even a little bit more than you thought you could, both in the moment and later on in the day with other tasks that require energy, too.

Another physics theory that applies to habit formation? Noether's theorem.[2] There's a lot I admittedly don't understand about the differences between momentum and (kinetic) energy, but the most important takeaway from this equation is that the more momentum you have, the more energy you have.

These connections to physics not only flesh out why baselines work (I'm just as surprised as you are!), they give us hope. Because the truth is that nobody wants to *only* have the smallest and simplest version of a habit for the rest of their lives. They want it to build.

Baselines Build-

If you're afraid to start with baselines because you think you will stay there, then I've got good news for you.

> **Thanks to the increasing energy that momentum provides, baselines build, and organically so.**
>
> BRAIN HACK

Translation: Baselines = Momentum = Organic growth.

But, this growth doesn't just apply to reaching your ideals—it applies to growing your baselines, too. As you move more toward

[2] John Baez, "Noether's Theorem in a Nutshell," 17 February 2020. https://math.ucr.edu/home/baez/noether.html.

your ideals, your highs get higher and your lows get higher, too.[3] This means that not only do your baselines naturally build up toward your ideals (yay!) but also whatever baseline version of your habit you can do on your worst day builds as well.

I mentioned when I first began my exercise habit after having my fifth baby that I started with 10 minutes of simply moving my body in any way that felt comfortable. After a few weeks of 10 minutes of gentle movement, my baseline started to naturally build both in time and in type. Eventually, my exercise baseline became 15 minutes for strength and 20 minutes for cardio. That's where it remains today, and I can fulfill my baseline even on my worst day. On more typical, but still ideal, days, I easily reach 30 minutes of strength and 30 minutes of cardio. (Note: this is not a prescription.)

My highs got higher, and my lows got higher, too.

These same results have been shared by literally hundreds of women:

- Anne, who sits for five minutes on her meditation cushion as a baseline, but more often does a 10–20 minute meditation.
- Kimber, who can at bare minimum walk around the block after seeing her daughter off on the school bus, but usually continues that walk to a nearby gym and completes a workout.
- Miranda, who can take one deep breath each morning after she wakes up, but typically completes about five minutes of deep breathing.
- Rosemarie, who at bare minimum can jot down some simple dinner ideas for the week, but most weeks plots out a full meal plan for her family—breakfasts, lunches, snacks, and dinners.

I know you want the ideal version of your habit. Baselines are the best way to get there. And, it will happen sooner than you think and be more sustainable than insisting on energy-sucking ideals.

---

[3] This is another Heroic Coaching principle I'll forever be thankful for.

Baselines Are Powerful–

Baselines are powerful; not just because they are the foundation to consistency and the building blocks for more, but because they have the power to support your life, like a net that is there to catch you when you fall.

One of my favorite Instagram comments I've ever received is from a user who wanted to share about her experience with baselines:

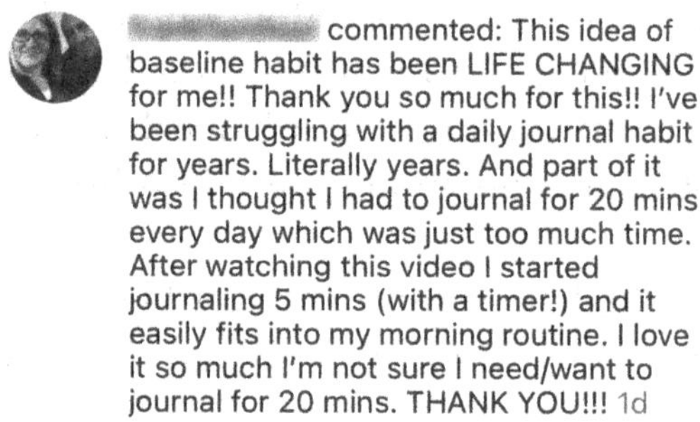

I've received dozens of other comments on baselines over the years. Don't underestimate the support that a baseline can provide. You may be like this commenter and find that your baseline is more than enough. (For example, my baseline for journaling just one line each night is honestly all I can muster most days.)

When you embrace the belief that habits are supportive, you can better allow yourself to believe that baselines are powerful just as they are.

Baselines are innately powerful. BRAIN HACK

More than Five Minutes

I coached a mom and full-time teacher named Rebecca who wanted to walk more regularly. The problem was that she had major hip and back issues she was receiving physical therapy for that limited her exercise. She also had both very little and varied time available to move, thanks to caretaking tasks after the school day ended that required her attention: getting her kids to extracurricular activities, cleaning, cooking, laundering, and so on.

First, we started with *why* walking would be supportive for Rebecca. Her answer was simple: walking most days would give Rebecca a mental break while also helping her body heal without hurting it. The most predictable time she could walk turned out to be during her prep period. Rebecca's ideal was to walk 30 minutes, so she decided on a baseline of walking 5 minutes around her school campus at the start of her break.

It made me smile to receive her check-in messages throughout the first week of implementation. Not only was Rebecca able to meet her baseline every day, I could hear in her voice a rising confidence in herself. After years of evidence that she thought proved otherwise, Rebecca was a regular walker. Rebecca excitedly told me about how she could do the baseline even if she had to prepare a lesson, or a kid showed up for help, or a colleague needed to meet. Those five minutes felt like so much more to Rebecca.

Thanks to the grounding peace and stability those five minutes provided, Rebecca was able to gradually build up to more walking minutes, and (I kid you not) even doing some strength training, all during her prep period. (As a super experienced teacher of a few decades, she thankfully didn't need much time to prep.) Rebecca couldn't have been happier about her now consistent exercise routine. But, my favorite part of the process was and is this: Rebecca proved her old self wrong.

Baselines make consistency possible, they create momentum, they build, and they are powerful. When you design your baseline to be small and simple, you have the right kind of baseline to change more than just your habits.

Form Your Own Baseline

As with all things habits, baselines are subjective. The key in selecting your habit, envisioning the ideal, then plotting the baseline is that it is all about *you*—what is good and right for you and your current season.

To assist you in forming your own baseline, I'll return to Sally Down the Street. I'll take each of Sally's ideals and turn them into versions she can do on her less-than-ideal days—in other words, baselines.

Sally Down the Street: Baselines

EXERCISE: I will go for a three-mile walk around my neighborhood in the a.m., after my kids go to school.

Three-mile walk → A walk around the block

SPIRITUAL PRACTICE: I will meditate 10 minutes in the early afternoon before the mad rush begins.

10-minute meditation → one minute of deep breathing

JOURNALING: I will write one page in my journal after I get ready for bed.

One page journaling → one line

Next: Make Your Habit Specific

With both the ideal and baseline versions of your selected habit in place, you can officially check off the supportive, small and simple rings of the Sticky Habit Matrix. But, to officially pass through the Sweet Spot, you need to hit the fourth and final ring: specific.

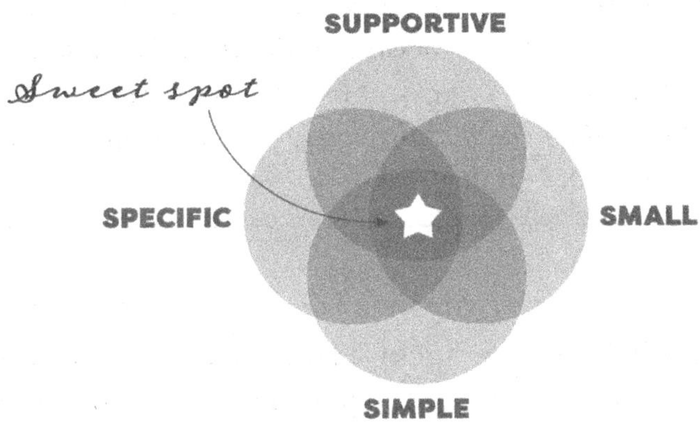

This is where the final pillar in phase one of the Sticky Habit Method comes in: Strategize. But first, how did Patrice do in forming a baseline?

PATRICE

Now that Patrice had set aside some family history time as a habit that could encompass scrapbooking to researching, she felt both excited and hesitant. After all, this work was deeply important to her, but also potentially never-ending. Patrice felt the pressure. I reminded her of why this habit was supportive for her—connection—and then asked Patrice to cast a vision of her ideal version of family history time. Patrice took a clarifying breath and was able to name it for herself: an hour of scrapbooking and/or researching her family tree. Already, by placing her habit in terms of time, Patrice felt more in control, like her

(continued)

(continued)

goal of connection was more possible regardless of how much she could get done within a frame of time. Then came the hard part—the smallest and simplest version of this—her baseline. Patrice took another moment, closed her eyes, and thought it through. She then opened her eyes and said with confidence, "10 minutes. Even on a bad or busy day, I can sit down and flip through my scrapbooks for 10 minutes." A sweet smile crept up on Patrice's face, one that clearly signaled both the relief and the surety she had long desired when it came to this valued habit.

TAKEAWAYS: The Sticky Habit Matrix entails four maxims of solid habit design, each as their own ring: supportive, small, simple, and specific. Where all those rings meet is the Sweet Spot. To make a supportive habit stick, cast a vision of your ideal, form a baseline version, and craft a specific strategy. Baselines contain built-in hacks that train your brain: they make consistency possible, create momentum, build, and are powerful. Strategizing a specific habit plan is next.

TAKE THOUGHT: What is the ideal version of the habit you selected? What is the smallest and simplest version, your baseline? What about baselines worry you? Excite you?

TAKE ACTION: Ensure your habit is supportive, small, and simple. Next, is the final ring of the Sticky Habit Matrix: Specific!

NOTE: For more (printables, recommended books, complementary podcast episodes, etc.), remember to check out the free and included Sticky Habit resources, available online at https://stickyhabitsbook.com/resources:

Chapter 8

Strategize

Learn: The third pillar of the Sticky Habit Method: Strategize a specific habit plan

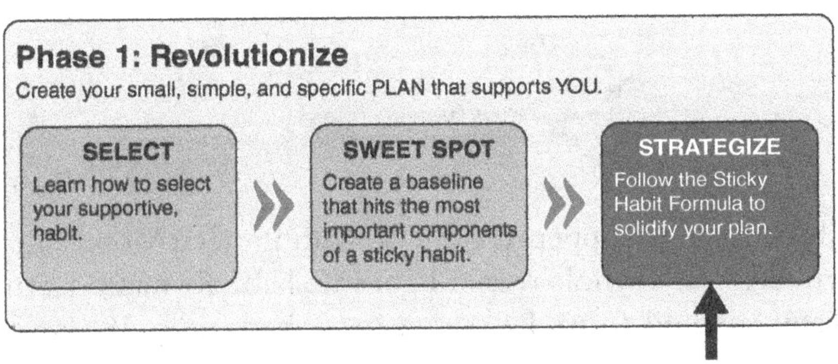

I was ecstatic. My little Instagram post about getting up earlier in the morning not only went "viral" by my novice estimation, it was going to CHANGE. THE. WORLD.

This challenge happened early on with Project: Monica Learns How to Sleep, the whole reason I got into habit formation. True to bro habit method form, I decided to embark on a 30-day habit challenge that combined both going to bed and waking up earlier. I named it the *Wake Up Early Challenge*. (I'm not known for creatively naming things, okay? I have other strengths . . . .)

In my excitement, I spontaneously made up a poster with my personal guidelines and posted it to Instagram, encouraging others to join me and commit via a comment. Then, my tiny little baby feed blew up. People were *all-in* on joining a challenge. They, too, were ready to change their sleeping habits. I was so thrilled by the outpouring of enthusiasm that I grew convinced that this could indeed change not just their habits, it could change *everything*.

I actually don't remember much of how the public challenge went. I have vague memories of forcing myself up in the dark, early morning hours, sharing a few progress posts, and getting gradually dissipating comments from people who were excited about their "progress," too. I remember hitting 21 out of the 30 days, something I felt sheepish about sharing since it was me who had organized the challenge in the first place, as if my lack of perfection made me a fraud.

Here's what I do remember quite clearly: the habit didn't stick. Not for me, and not for the hundreds turned tens of people who crawled over the finish line alongside me.

You Need a Real Habit Plan

There was a lot wrong with this challenge. Can you name a few things?

When I was an overachieving perfectionist, the "Start Monday" mindset reigned supreme. I would start *all* the things, all at the same time, and all with the ideal versions on . . . you guessed it . . . Monday. We've already identified many issues with this approach, primarily being that it's just too much to be realistically sustainable. One other big reason why this mindset sets women up to fail is that Start Monday habits are what I call *dangling habits*. Remember the Dangler Habiteer, when habits are not specific enough to stick?

Nothing about this challenge was specific. Sure, it *looks* clear enough. But, in truth, my litany of rules were pulled out of thin air and executed much the same way. I was supposed to "just do it" with my high motivation leading the way and my gritty self-control making it happen day after day until I reached nirvana.

Let me be bold: deciding on a start day is not a strategy. Having rules that aren't grounded in reality is not a strategy. Forcing a habit to magically appear without attaching it to an already-existing habit is not a strategy. Hitting everything all at once is not a strategy. Going right for the ideal is not a strategy. Thirty days straight (or even 21/28/100 days) is not a strategy.

So, what is??

You need a specific habit plan. And doing so helps you hit the Sweet Spot by filling the fourth and final ring of the Sticky Habit Matrix: Specific.

A Formula for Habits

This won't surprise you: I'm not a mathematician. Thanks to my nerdy friends and their positive peer pressure, I was all but carried against my will into honors and A.P. math classes in high school, passed the big test, then never took a math class again. Six months after scoring a 4 on the A.P. Calculus exam, I found myself in a college Freshman nutrition class test struggling to remember what 6×4 is.

This is all to say that "me + math" do not, well, math.

Keep this in mind when I tell you that there *is* an equation to crafting a habit plan. And if I am going to provide it to you, then you really better listen up. Good news: there are no numbers involved; just timing. Also more good news: you've already learned 2/3rd of this.

The Sticky Habit Formula:

W + T + A = Sticky Habit

Let's break that down some more, shall we? I'll go step-by-step, gradually expanding on each.

W: *WHEN* (an already existing habit)

T: *THEN* (your new baseline habit)

A: *AFTER* (a healthy dose of positive reinforcement)

(Psst: this is the first you're hearing about this step—stay tuned)

When-Then Pairing

Once you cast a vision of your ideal habit and form a baseline version, then you need to get strategic (read: Specific) by using the Sticky Habit Formula. The most overlooked step is the first half of the When-Then Pairing: *WHEN*.

You may not believe this, but you already have habits. You simply may not acknowledge this fact because they're indeed habits. You don't have to think about them. You don't have to try. You don't have to expend much energy. They simply happen.

Don't believe me? Then answer these questions:

- Do you wash your hands after using the bathroom? (Please say yes.)
- Do you start the dishwasher?
- Do you get dressed?
- Do you wake up around a typical time?
- Do you brush your teeth?
- Do you look at your phone when it buzzes?

These (plus hundreds more) are habits. You *are* a habit person after all!

All (and I really mean *all*) of us have rhythms to our days, ones that are defined by *what* we need to do and *where* we need to be during certain timeframes. These are the kinds of habits that become your *WHEN* in the When-Then Pairing. It's classic habit stacking, y'all—one of the habit bro method tips that transcends gender.

In his book *The Power of Habit,* investigative journalist and author Charles Duhigg breaks down why habit stacking works: it's brain science.[1] All behaviors come from cues (internal or external), meaning triggers from our environment, brain, and body that lead

---

[1] Charles Duhigg, *The Power of Habit: Why We Do What We Do in Life and Business* (Random House, 2014).

to us automatically doing/thinking/feeling something (i.e., a habit). Then, each of these behaviors is rewarded through physical sensations or emotional payoffs, the kind that tell your brain to seek out more of the behaviors that preceded them. This pattern can be hacked and replicated to create and amend habits.[2] This brain hack is the foundation of the Sticky Habit Formula. We simply get intentional about how to use this already existing habit pattern to our benefit as we intentionally form new ones.

Habits exist in patterns with triggers before and rewards after. Design your new habits using the Sticky Habit Formula.

BRAIN HACK

I recommend the following steps once you're ready for the Implementation stage (coming up!). The first three steps we've already covered are italicized:

1. *Select a habit.*
2. *Cast a vision of your ideal version of this habit.*
3. *Form a baseline version.*
4. Strategize a specific habit plan:
   a. Think about the general time of day this habit (ideal or baseline) would need to take place.
   b. Then, recall what existing habits you already have during this time. (Need ideas? Check out the Sticky Habit Formula Cheat Sheet included in your free online resources.)
   c. Decide on one existing habit that makes the most sense for you and *make it as specific as possible*. You've got your *WHEN*!

That final step is key. If you want to do something after you're done cleaning up breakfast, then what is typically the last action of cleaning? If you want to insert a new habit at bedtime, what is a

[2] Stay tuned for Part Five, where we'll apply this pattern to revising our bad habits.

current behavior from that time of day—a habit—that you could attach the new one to? Without specifics, our habits remain *dangling*—and we want them *attached.*

That same specificity needs to be applied to your *THEN*, which I would write down as the baseline version of the habit you want. The main reason for that is simply because the baseline is where you'll typically start when you install a new habit, and we want a crystal clear WTA (*WHEN* + *THEN* + *AFTER*) forming your habit plan.

Your specific *WHEN* coupled with your *THEN* (your baseline habit) is your official When-Then Pairing. And it's how you can form a habit that sticks. The When-Then Pairing is precise enough that it acts as a game-changing tool for many women.

Taryn attached her Taryn Time habit to one she already had: eating lunch. She got really specific about how she'd know she was done: placing her plate in the sink. Her When-Then Pairing looked like this: *WHEN* I put my dish in the sink, *THEN* I'll walk back to my office to take Taryn Time. The office location was key to Taryn because it was the place in the home she could call her own, and where she goes anyway after lunch to return to work. By combining her already existing patterns with a new habit, Taryn was better prepared to get started.

To give you some ideas now without having to look it up online, here are a few of the *WHEN*s you can pull from to attach to your *THEN*s. (This comes from the Sticky Habit Cheat Sheet, a printable you can download for free at https:stickyhabitsbook.com/resources.)

When

» Finish brushing my teeth.
» Close/start the dishwasher.
» End my workout.
» Step out of the shower.
» Place dish in sink.
» Get into bed.
» Brush my hair.
» End breakfast.
» Wash my hands.
» Start the car.
» Flush the toilet.
» Finish my prayers.
» Unload the dishwasher.
» End lunch.
» Clear the table.
» Park the car.
» End dinner.
» Get ready.
» Wash the dishes.
» Put on my pajamas.
» Finish exercising.
» Wash my face.
» Turn off my alarm.
» Get out of bed.
» Wait in line.
» Turn on the car.
» Prep a meal.
» Put on makeup.
» Get on my shoes.
» Say goodnight.

We're not done forming your habit plan yet. After all, the formula is WT*A*. So, what's the *A*? It's the most underestimated but arguably most important step of all, and it may be the very thing that completely changes not just the way you behave, but the way you *see* yourself.

After

If you've ever potty trained a child or a dog, then you already know the power of positive reinforcement. From sticker charts to tummy rubs, encouraging good behavior by rewarding that behavior is not a form of manipulation but of brain science. Behaviors create neural pathways in our brains and the ones that instigate pleasure in the form of happy chemicals (like serotonin, oxytocin, endorphins, and dopamine) construct pathways that get good and deep, real fast. You can access those happy chemicals and established brain pathways in a few ways *after you've* completed a habit via a form of positive reinforcement. This is another brain hack!

To make habits really stick, use forms of positive reinforcement that create the happy chemicals your brain craves.

BRAIN HACK

I learned this as a new middle school teacher. Before becoming a mom, I taught English and history in urban-suburban middle schools in the Oakland, California area. During my first year, I felt certain that to be a respected and effective instructor I needed to jump on any sign of misbehavior and mold my students via strict-but-fair discipline (aka consequences), helping them learn to behave in ways that were appropriate to my classroom. I found this model to be both incredibly taxing and inconsistent in outcomes.

In my second year of teaching, I was lucky to be under the mentorship of an experienced teacher. She taught me something that went against all I thought I knew about discipline, yet completely transformed my efficacy as a teacher: reward the *good* as much as possible.

I did this via positive reinforcement in a variety of ways:

- As I waited for the students to quiet down or get out their materials, instead of calling out the kids who were not doing what they were supposed to, I called out the kids who *were*. (This required a level of self-control I didn't know I had.)
- During focused work times, I silently placed small prize tokens on the desk of each student clearly doing their assignment—tokens that could be used as money to purchase fun things from our class store a few times a month. (Yes, middle schoolers are basically giant toddlers and love stickers, prizes, and praise.)
- Each class period received points for collectively engaging in ways that benefitted the whole, points that earned regular rewards like class parties.

Of course, there were still times and students that needed specific traditional discipline with consequences for misbehavior, but those times became rare because overall they found it felt so very good to be noticed for doing well and trying hard.

This shift in using positive reinforcement as my main form of classroom management not only changed my teaching, it also went on to transform both my parenting and eventually the way I learned to parent myself. It's something that I can drift away from, but I always come back to positive reinforcement because it works.

How to Use Positive Reinforcement When Paired with New Habits

There are a variety of ways that the Good Men with Great Methods have used this positive reinforcement pattern in their habit models.

Charles Duhigg suggests a literal reward when you follow through with a new habit, like filling in a habit tracker or having a piece of chocolate. (I myself am very fond of rewarding myself by watching a YouTube video of couples renovating abandoned British manors.) James Clear advises people to make the habit rewarding in and of itself.[3] BJ Fogg narrows in on literal celebrations, like pumping your fist, giving yourself a high five, and basking in the feel-good feelings.[4]

These are all good and worth thinking through. However, I've found that regardless of the form of positive reinforcement, it's essential that it not only affirms the behavior but also your *identity*. This is something that professional athletes and their coaches know and use to their benefit.

Lanny Bassham is an American sport shooter who won silver and later gold medals at the 1972 and 1976 Olympic games, respectively, alongside many, many other accolades. After his initial Olympic silver win, Bassham was eager to know how to get himself over the tipping point to extra excellence, and he believed it came down to his mental game.

Mental performance training was hard to find in the 1970s—people weren't really into studying nor teaching about how your thoughts affect your physical performance. So, Bassham decided to find out for himself how the best athletes' mental game played into their athletic success. He was disgruntled to discover that the elites declared that the game is 90% mental, but they were training mentally just 10% of the time. Bassham wanted to make some changes to that latter percentage, so he created the Mental Management System, and went on for several decades teaching and coaching people pursuing excellence from sports to pageantry, starting with training how they *thought*.[5]

---

[3] We already chatted about this when selecting your habit and how to make it both desirable and feel-good (James Clear, *Atomic Habits: An Easy & Proven Way to Build Good Habits & Break Bad Ones* [Avery, 2018]).

[4] BJ Fogg, *Tiny Habits: The Small Changes That Change Everything* (Harvest, 2021).

[5] Lanny Bassham, *With Winning in Mind*, 3rd ed. (Mental Management Systems, 2012).

In his book, *With Winning in Mind*, Bassham fleshes out perhaps the most make-it-or-break-it habit of the mind: **self-image**. One of the key ways Bassham has helped so many accomplish such great things is by molding their identity and boosting it wherever they can with three simple words: **"That's like me."**[6]

He advised entrepreneurs and Olympians alike to declare this statement *every* single time they saw themselves behaving in a way that aligned with the way they *wanted* to see themselves, from hitting a target to calming down nerves to finishing a hard workout. I have found these three words act as both the simplest and the most effective form of positive reinforcement in habit formation because (1) the mantra is a literal affirmation that acts as a positive reinforcement—a win-win—and (2) it hits at the heart of what I believe is the most underused tool in behavior and habit design: *identity*.

The Missing Piece in Habit Design: Identity

If you've ever been lucky to be under the care of a great cognitive therapist or life coach like I have, then you are well familiar with how our thoughts tie into our behaviors. In my life and my work with helping women mold their lives, I've adopted a version of this pattern as a coach, but with an identity-centered twist. It looks like this:

[6] I first learned about Bassham and "That's like me" in my Heroic Coaching training.

In short: the way we behave affects the way we see ourselves, and the way we see ourselves shapes the way we behave. This is a behavior pattern that becomes a cycle in thought and in action.

This cycle can be used in two main ways: for good or for bad. I'll break it all down far more for you in Chapter 11, but here's what you need to know about this cycle right now: just as much as you're working to reinforce a behavior, you're working to change the way you see yourself.

The more you reward your behavior, the better it'll stick; and the more that reward is about *who* you are, not just what you do, the better the behavior *and* the identity will stick, too.

The best forms of positive reinforcement tie back to identity. BRAIN HACK

I've seen this play out well in woman after woman, client after client. Take Olivia for example, whose long-standing issues with attention deficit hyperactivity disorder (ADHD) convinced her that she never follows through. As she worked to prioritize taking a moment of stillness each night after putting her kids to bed, she would tell herself, "I can follow through." With time, she saw herself more and more capable of doing so in many other areas of her life.

Katie also comes to mind, a woman self-charged with managing her husband's neurodiverse needs alongside their household. Katie struggled to manage the inflow of mail, forms, and bills that piled up, interfering with the ongoing care she was providing for her spouse. This lack of a system also created problems as she oversaw building their new home. Once we got a clear When-Then Pairing, each Friday after her five minutes of going through papers and jotting down to-dos, Katie chose to say to herself, "I did it!" Not only did her confidence grow in acting as the chief operating officer of their home, but also in seeing herself as someone who can manage spinning plates well.

Finally, I think of Rebecca, the teacher I mentioned in Chapter 7. More times than not, as she fit in her baseline of a five-minute walk at the beginning of her prep period, she not only pumped her fist and said "That's like me!" but she also felt the pride of it, too. With time, that growing identity helped her expand her regular workouts into other forms of consistent self-care.

When you design your *AFTER*, regardless of whether it's a literal reward, an action, a feeling, or a mantra, you'll find it even more reinforcing if you tie it back to the way you see yourself. One woman named Andrea had this to say about the identity piece as she reported on how her habit was going: "After finishing and saying 'That's like me!' it really did *feel* like me."

Some women have found they like to take the identity step even further and do their own version of "That's like me!" but with a true identity focus, like "I'm a runner," "I'm a journaler," or "I'm a meal prepper." But even absent a specific title, "That's like me" connects back to the core of who we truly want to be. That's why Taryn chose it as her *AFTER* to the WTA for Taryn Time. It was both easy and effective.

This identity-centered transformation has been replicated time and time again, and Patrice was no different.

PATRICE

Patrice was ready *to officially install her new habit. After thinking through the time of day she wanted her family history time—the morning—she carefully crafted her own habit plan following the Sticky Habit Formula. Her WTA looked like this:* "WHEN *I finish cleaning up breakfast by putting the dishes away,* THEN *I'll spend 10 minutes on family history time,* AFTER *I'll say 'I'm a memory keeper!' and 'I am a finisher!'" With some trepidation,*

(continued)

(continued)

Patrice set forth. The biggest thing holding her back? Her own track record of falling off the wagon.

Patrice felt unsure if this habit would be like all the others. Perhaps it would prove all the fears true she had long carried about herself: "I'm lazy. I don't follow through. I lack self-discipline." But, Patrice chose to have the "greatest of courage" and to try anyway, to try in a different way. With the extra challenge from me to do just *the baseline for the first few times, Patrice told herself that she could do this. And do it, she did. Not only was Patrice successful in installing her baseline habit, it also soon grew toward that ideal more times than not. Patrice was thrilled to have the habit, but she was even more excited to have a new perspective on who she is and what she is capable of.*

Patrice was part of a small online group I was teaching the SHM to. Here's what she had to say after the final day of her Four-Day Sprint (which you'll learn about soon!):

> *"I completed day four and I am so proud of myself! I woke up today with some strong anxiety because my brain was saying, 'You never finish anything. You can't finish the Four-Day Sprint.' I started to feel stuck and paralyzed, but thankfully I got through the anxiety, recognizing that my brain needs to be rewired. I did my WTA, and then with both arms in the air and tears in my eyes I said,* 'I am a memory keeper! I am a finisher!!' "

Patrice later described the full experience as "life changing."

I know the truth. It wasn't the family history time that changed Patrice's life—although I'm sure it's a wonderful form of connection and purpose for her. What changed for Patrice was that rewiring. She was able to prove her old identities—her old fears about herself—wrong. Patrice gained new evidence that supported the way she truly wants to see herself, her *true* self. And this was just the beginning for Patrice to continue to do that, both in thought and in action.

I've said it before and I'll say it again: habits go deeper.

Finalize Your WTA

Are you ready to design your A of the Sticky Habit Formula? Once you've decided your When-Then Pairing, you also need to settle on a reasonable A (*AFTER*), which should be a form of positive reinforcement. I'll share some examples next pulling from the Sticky Habit Cheat Sheet included in your online resources, but do you want the simplest one? Say, "That's like me!" (Thanks, Lanny!)

Affirm

- Say, "That's like me!"
- Smile.
- Clap your hands.
- Take a deep breath.
- Say, "Woohoo!!!"
- Put a bead in a jar.
- Do a little dance.
- Feel proud.
- Say, "Good job!"
- Put a mark on your habit tracker.
- Give yourself a pat on the back.
- Light a candle.
- Say, "I did it!"
- Place your hands on your heart.
- Do a "Tiger Woods" fist pump.
- Play a happy song on your smart speaker.
- "Pump it up" with your hands.
- Declare, "I am a Revolutionizer!"
- Text accountability buddy a thumbs up.
- Roar!

A few quick notes about *AFTER*: even a baseline warrants an *AFTER*, including if you've long passed that beginning phase and are having a baseline day. Also, while it's *so* important that you reinforce the new habit every single time for a while, you won't be stuck doing that the rest of your life. The *AFTER* will organically fall away,[7] but the compassionate, affirming mindset will remain.

[7] In *Tiny Habits*, BJ Fogg teaches this about his celebration step, and I've found it true for any form of positive reinforcement used as the *AFTER* step in a WTA.

So, what's your WTA? (If you're stuck, remember to reference the Sticky Habit Cheat Sheet located in the free online resources found at https://stickyhabitsbook.com/resources.)

Before you make your own WTA, I'd like to return to Sally Down the Street and what clear WTAs could look like for her.

Sally Down the Street: WTAs

EXERCISE: Walking in morning, with a baseline of a walk around the block

WHEN I return from dropping the kids off at school,
+ *THEN* I will go for a walk around the block,
+ *AFTER* I will say, "That's like me!"

SPIRITUAL PRACTICE: Meditation in early afternoon, with a baseline of one minute of breathing

WHEN I finish loading the dishwasher after lunch,
+ *THEN* I will do one minute of deep breathing,
+ *AFTER* I will fill in my habit tracker.

JOURNALING: Writing in journal at night, with the baseline of one line

WHEN I finish brushing my teeth and arrive at my bed,
+ *THEN* I will write one line in my journal,
+ *AFTER* I will light my favorite candle as a reward while I read what I wrote.

Do you have a clear WTA now? If so, congratulations! You strategized your specific habit plan, thus filling the final ring of the Sticky Habit Matrix—you've hit the Sweet Spot!

Now, you are ready to move on to Implementation, which is the first pillar under phase two of the Sticky Habit Method. Already worried about failing? Don't be! Like we learned, making mistakes is all part of implementing a new habit. I'll teach you what to do about those failures, too.

TAKEAWAYS: Fill the final ring of the Sticky Habit Matrix (thereby hitting the Sweet Spot) by strategizing a specific habit plan. Mimic the natural pattern habits follow with the Sticky Habit Formula (WTA: *WHEN* + *THEN* + *AFTER*). Decide a When-Then Pairing for your new habit (habit stacking!), and how you plan to reinforce it afterward. Identity is a missing piece in habit design, so consider adopting "That's like me!" as your go-to *AFTER*.

TAKE THOUGHT: What is an existing habit you can attach your new baseline habit to? How have you seen forms of positive reinforcement improve your performance AND how you see yourself? What do you think you'll do for the *AFTER* step of the Sticky Habit Formula?

TAKE ACTION: Strategize a WTA for your new habit. This is your habit plan!

NOTE: For more (printables, recommended books, complementary podcast episodes, etc.), remember to check out the free and included Sticky Habit resources, available online at https://stickyhabitsbook.com/resources:

Part Four

REFINE: PHASE TWO OF THE STICKY HABIT METHOD

Habit Story 3

Name: Sarah

Responsibilities: Stay-at-home mom to seven children including some with special needs, overseeing a home renovation, and doing lots of the work herself

Habit fail: Getting ready

Sarah was embarrassed to admit it, but she would end most days feeling as frazzled as she looked. This wasn't new. As a mom to seven kids (yes, she knows that's a lot of kids), many of whom are neurodiverse, Sarah had long felt like each day took all she had to give. But now, life was even more chaotic thanks to renovating their new home nearby so they could move in. Sarah and her husband were not only acting as contractor overseeing all the moving parts to their renovation but also Sarah—with her great creative gifts—often needed to be at the house, designing, painting, and curating a home that reflected the way she hoped her children would feel being raised in it. This artistic talent applied to all areas of her life, except one: getting herself ready for the day. Sarah used to love expressing herself through her clothes, hair, and accessories, but this priority had fallen off the list completely. In fact, not only was Sarah not getting "ready-ready" but she also wasn't even showering, brushing her hair, or taking care of her teeth. As she kept waiting for the "right" and "full" time to get ready, she kept on waiting and even basic hygiene slipped away. Sarah knew it wasn't about the way she looked; *it was about the way she* felt. *If she could ensure she was prioritizing caring for herself by getting herself ready—just like she does for everyone else—she would feel more like Sarah and better able to tackle the endless responsibilities her life holds. But, the biggest question for Sarah was "How?"*

This question of how has been halfway answered via phase one of the Sticky Habit Method. Up to this point, you've learned how to redefine habits and revolutionize how you form them, including coming up with your habit plan (WTA). Now, with phase two comes the implementation of that plan as you honor, tweak, and build your baseline.

Chapter 9

Implement

Learn: The fourth pillar of the Sticky Habit Method: install your habit plan by following the Implementation Cycle

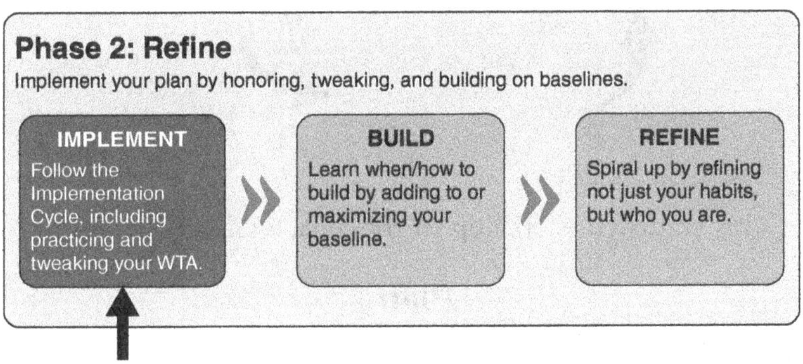

I grew up on the foothills of the Rocky Mountains, with parents who loved to hike. Thanks to tagging along (not always willingly), I often saw the water cycle up close. While heading down the mountains, we could see how water that began in trickles at the top gradually gathered into small streams, with rushing creeks at the bottom. Not only did seeing this firsthand help me understand my science lessons on how water goes from condensation to precipitation to evaporation on repeat (a simplified version, I know—but, like math, my science knowledge essentially stopped at eighth grade), I could see how everything in nature happens cyclically.

Habits are no different. There is a cycle to implementing our habit plans, and the goal in doing so is to flow through this cycle, like water does in nature. Just like you can't snap your fingers and go from raindrops to reservoirs, your habit plan will need to move through a series of steps to become a real bona fide habit—the kind you don't have to think about.

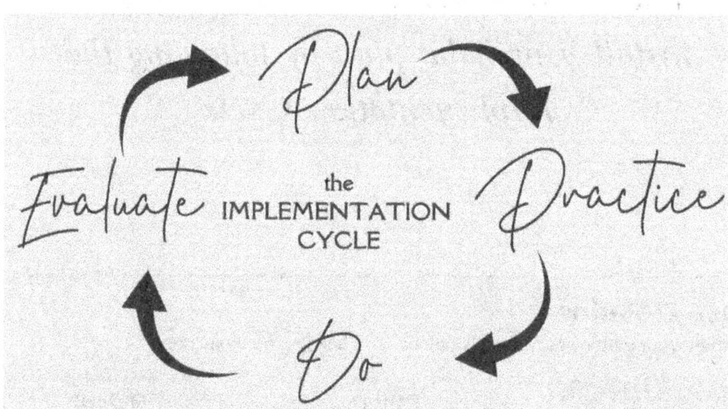

Let's break down each step of this process.

Plan

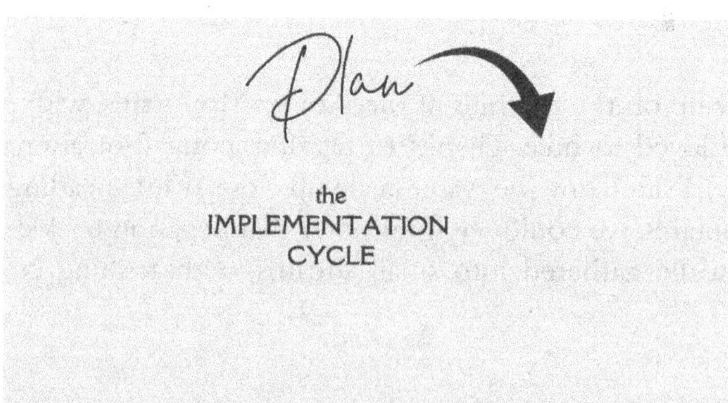

Good news! You know this step, as you've already done it. To form your habit plan, you select your habit, cast a vision of the ideal, form a baseline version, and strategize a habit plan—your WTA (*WHEN + THEN + AFTER*).

SARAH

*Sarah selected a habit of getting ready in the morning, with her ideal including a shower and teeth brushed, hair and makeup done, and a cute outfit to boot. As her baseline, Sarah chose hygiene and clean clothes, something she could do in less than five minutes on an extra busy day. She then crafted a WTA by deciding on her When-Then Pairing (*WHEN *I wake up,* THEN *I'll immediately get ready) with a simple* AFTER *of "That's like me!" Her WTA was complete. This process involved being realistic about her season of life and choosing to prioritize getting ready over working out (something she wanted to do but found she was stuck in workout clothes all day, ultimately neither working out nor getting ready!). Sarah had to make a trade-off, acknowledging that this busy season of running between houses and doing a lot of physical labor was exercise enough, and she would feel better if she did so with a minimum of good hygiene along for the ride.*

Practice

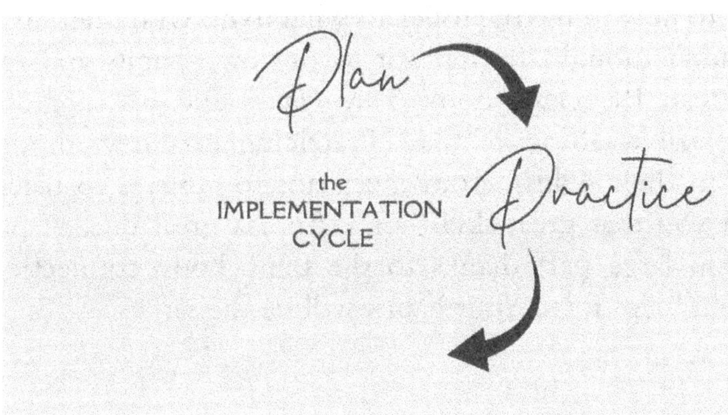

We all may know what it means to practice, especially when it comes to new skill sets like learning an instrument, but have you ever *practiced* a new habit? The practice step of the Implementation Cycle is where you run through your WTA outside of real time, creating a beneficial brain-body connection that will help your habit stick.

Brain-Body Connection

It's not new science that the brain and body are connected, but most of us don't use that as a learning tool. The concept here is to take something that the brain is studying (like a new skill or a set of facts) and then form connections from the brain *to* the body.

This brain-body connection is something I used as a teacher at the beginning of each semester to train my students on our usual routines, like how to enter the classroom and get started on first tasks. Instead of drilling the steps into them with only verbal repetition, I assigned body movements to represent each task. We would pantomime the order over and over until it became second nature. By the third day of school, my students could perfectly follow through with our routines without me having to say a word. Their bodies simply knew what to do, like how to enter the classroom, grab their notebooks, sit down and answer that day's journaling prompt.

I've used this same principle time after time with my own small children as they learned things from the family nighttime routine, to how to use the toilet, to what to do with their dirty dish.

I hadn't thought to apply it to my own habits and routines until I read BJ Fogg's book *Tiny Habits* and his suggestion to rehearse habits ahead of time. Practicing isn't new though. All experts in their fields—from musicians to athletes to teachers—will tell you that great skills come from a great deal of practice. This is in large part thanks to the brain-body connection that practicing helps form. Your habits will be the same.

Practice Your WTA

With your habit plan in hand—your WTA—you need to *practice* that series of steps outside of real time. Imagine you are an actor quickly blocking out where you're supposed to be on stage before curtain time; it's like that! This will help your brain and body make deeper connections so you will rely less on willpower and remembering your habit. Instead, it will feel automatic.

Practicing your habit helps create a brain-body connection that reinforces the behavior, so it will feel more natural in real time. BRAIN HACK

I'll be honest: you will feel dumb practicing. But, it really works. Here's how I recommend doing so.

Pretend it's the time of day when you will be doing your new habit, and put your body in that place. What's your *WHEN*? Quickly act like you're finishing that step. What's your *THEN*? Pretend you're doing your baseline (again, like an actor blocking out a part, so not the full thing). Finally, what's your *AFTER*? Act out the positive reinforcement you have planned. This whole practicing process should take far less time than actually doing it, typically less than a minute.

In line with Fogg's recommendations,[1] it's wise to practice your WTA three to five times in a row. Again, this will solidify the whole series of steps so your brain is more likely to remember the habit when it's go time. This has been true for each client who has dared to feel a little dumb and practice, then reaped the benefits of doing so. Like Jodee, who said, *"I sat up this morning to get out of bed and it was crazy how my brain and body was programmed to hit the floor and go do what I had practiced: walk to my closet, kneel, and pray. Wow!"*

---

[1]BJ Fogg, *Tiny Habits: The Small Changes That Change Everything* (Harvest, 2021).

Other Benefits to Practicing

There are two more benefits to practicing. One is that you can catch what doesn't work. This is what Natalie had to say about that advantage as she was working on using her phone less at night by plugging it in at a certain time, far away from where she'd be tempted to use it:

> *"Doing a practice run has helped me tweak my WTA. It brought out a couple logistical challenges, like the fact that I can't rely on my phone charger always being in the office, because my teenagers make off with chargers left out there! So, I've adjusted my WTA to simply 'plug-in phone' wherever I can and I'm hopeful things will go more smoothly because of this dry run."*

Another benefit worth mentioning is that while most women simply practice their WTA in one round, others have found it helpful to run through it again if the habit is shaky, they forget it in real time, or they come back to it after some time away.

Patrice from Part Three found practicing her family history time extra helpful in building her confidence as she learned this new way of forming habits. When the fear-driven voices in her head told her she couldn't install her new habit, she practiced again. *"I practiced today with my WTA about six times because I could feel the benefit, and by the fourth time I was so happy that I cried happy tears! I would not have believed how important this step was unless I tried it myself."*

In case you haven't heard it from me in a while, the Sticky Habit Method (SHM) is a new habit method and some steps will feel outside of the norm. This practicing step is something I advise every newcomer to SHM to do. Over time, you may find you don't need to practice every new habit—but I can guarantee it will help any habit you want to be stickier. It's worth the three to five minutes it requires.

I've had women who follow each part of the SHM, *except* the practice step. When they finally do, they see the value. Like Megan, who said,

"My dangling habits aren't so dangly anymore . . . . Because of that practice step that I always skipped before, I find myself naturally walking to where I need to be, even if I think I don't want to. I never thought I'd be good at habits because I do have memory issues and distraction issues. I'm actually hopeful now!"

This initial uncertainty turned aha! was shared by Sarah:

SARAH

Sarah looked a little skeptical as she learned about the practice step, but she decided it was worth a try. So, after our call she went to her bedroom, hesitated before getting in her bed, but got in anyway. Sarah then quickly pretended she woke up, walked straight into her bathroom, mimed washing her face, brushing her teeth, and putting on clean clothes. She then said, "That's like me!" It took less than a minute, so she shrugged her shoulders and did it all two more times. The next morning, when Sarah woke up she was shocked to find how her body went into autopilot and moved right into her get-ready habit. Maybe this practicing thing works after all?

Do

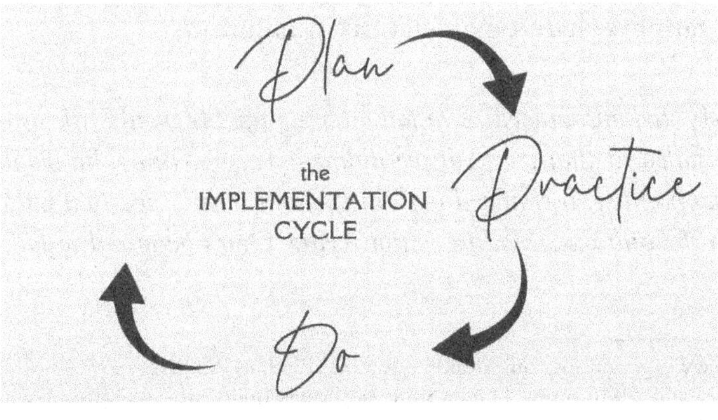

This may be obvious, but now your job is to actually *do* your new habit. However, there are some not-so-obvious elements to this phase that I want you to be aware of, plus a suggestion.

Expect Failure as Part of the Process

First is this: expect imperfection. While having a specific plan and practicing that plan sets you up for more success, you will likely find that actually doing the habit poses some unforeseen obstacles, from inner resistance to finding out your baseline is not baseline enough.

Proceed with curiosity. The whole point of this phase is not perfection, it's discovery. What works about your WTA? What doesn't? Noting these answers with an objective interest is what will help you move forward in informed ways, rather than a hypercritical manner that honestly dooms you to quit.

Expecting failure isn't apathy, it's expertise. As we talked about the growth mindset in Chapter 5, world-class teachers, athletes, musicians, businesspeople, and parents alike expect that failure is part of the process. Yo-Yo Ma, arguably the most famous cellist of all time, speaks often on the importance of accepting mistakes even amid the highest level of performance: "If you are only worried about not making a mistake then you will communicate nothing."[2] Sarah Blakely, founder of Spanx and self-made billionaire, said this of her family's shared expectation of failure:

> *"My dad encouraged us to fail growing up. He would ask us what we failed at that week. If we didn't have something, he would be disappointed. It changed my mindset at an early age that failure is not the outcome—failure is not trying. Don't be afraid to fail."*[3]

---

[2] https://www.goodreads.com/author/quotes/231708.Yo_Yo_Ma?

[3] Rose Leadem, "9 Inspiring Quotes from Self-Made Billionaire and Spanx Founder Sara Blakely." *Entrepreneur*, 12 September 2018. https://www.entrepreneur.com/leadership/9-inspiring-quotes-from-self-made-billionaire-and-spanx/319539?

Carrying the expectation of failure is ultimately what sets us all up for success in the long run. Someone who embraces failure as part of the process also knows that the real goal is to learn, to tweak (coming up), and to improve over time, because success is never really overnight.

Your messy attempts at a new habit aren't a reflection of your ineptness; they are part of the process.

One thing I tell my coaching clients all the time is, "**In the trying is the doing.**" That's really what matters in this phase—less that you do the habit perfectly, and more that you are *trying*.

> **In the trying is the doing.**

Another thing to note: you may not "feel" like it. Typically around the practice phase, if not before, many women lose the initial spark of excitement brought by the new habit. This is a human tendency. I often think of when I was a piano teacher on the side and my seven-year-old student who arrived at her first lesson with a level-10 excitement. However, by the third lesson she burst into tears, lamenting, "This isn't fun anymore!"

This is why we start with baselines, so we can focus on creating momentum instead of waiting for motivation. If your baseline isn't easy enough to do when you don't feel like it, it needs to be smaller and simpler. And if that's the case, in the words of Stuart Smalley, "That's okay!"

Training Your Brain That Baselines Count

Speaking of baselines: you are training your brain to believe that baselines count. If you design a solid baseline but never, ever let yourself *just* do the baseline, then on a true baseline day your brain is *not* going to believe you. So, you'll either not do any form of the habit and thereby lose your consistency (and the habit), or you'll insist on the ideal, which will eventually also cost you your consistency (burnout, anyone?). Or another area of your life may pay the price of the ideal, from your energy to your relationships.

To train your brain to believe that baselines count, stick *only* to your baseline for the first few times while installing your new habit. BRAIN HACK

With this first go especially, please trust me and be forceful about *only* doing your baseline. Our old all-or-nothing brains need to be trained to accept that doing *something* counts. And the more you do *something*, the more you'll add not only to your consistency, but to the building potential that will make your habit highs higher, and your habit lows higher, too. (Remember, baselines build!)

Four-Day Sprint

Finally: I recommend dedicating a few days to intentionally install your new habit, and initially, just the one. That way you can learn this new habit formation method and gain the skill sets required before installing more than one habit at a time. That singular focus also gives this habit even more sticky potential, *and* you train your brain with the baseline version so on true baseline days, your brain will believe you when you say, "Just the baseline today."

I suggest doing this in what I call the ***Four-Day Sprint***. It's simple: decide which day you will start, practice your WTA three to five times ahead of the first day, then move through four days with your full WTA, focusing only on the baseline for the first day or two.

You won't be stuck forever doing a Four-Day Sprint every time you install a new habit. But, it's *very* wise to do so when first using the SHM so you can develop some sticky habit muscles.

A Four-Day Sprint is also wise when approaching a trickier habit, perhaps with its own history of failure, or if it's super important right now. Imagine you are approaching a season where you have to have an earlier wakeup time. Doing a Four-Day Sprint a few weeks in advance of the actual switch and working up to the earlier time is a great way to make it both easier and more sustainable.

Each time I've taught the SHM in an intensive setting with a small group of women, I've witnessed the power of the Four-Day Sprint. Honestly, it can be a bit of an emotional roller coaster, as if this short period of time acts as a nucleus to what a broader habit life involves: excitement, intention, planning, resistance, obstacles, self-doubt, frustration, persistence, adapting, and, ultimately, triumph.

Do you remember Patrice, our case study from Part Three? Her thrill and pride with finishing the Four-Day Sprint exemplifies how transformative it can be. She went from being a "non-finisher" to being a "memory keeper." But that transition involved some frustration, fear, and fixing her WTA. In the trying is the doing, and the Four-Day Sprint is the ultimate space to try.

Next comes the tweaking. (Nope, not twerking—tweaking. That could have been really awkward.)

Evaluate and Tweak

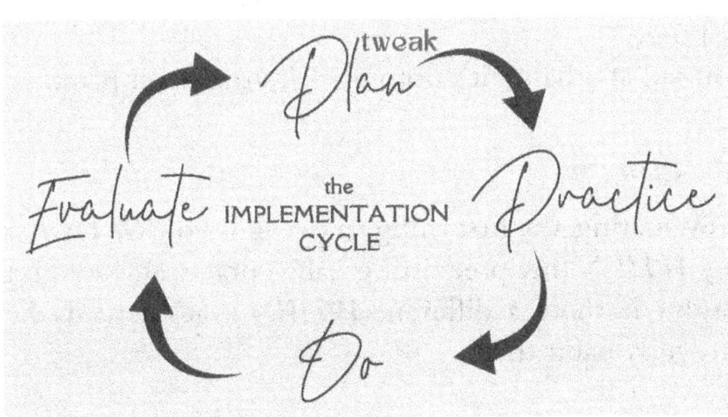

Here's where you get to act as a habit scientist and get objective about what doesn't work with your WTA, what unforeseen obstacles get in your way, and how you choose to tweak your WTA so you can continue to move through the Implementation Cycle. (Yes, you may need a few rounds.)

Evaluating how your habit is functioning can happen as you go, like during your Four-Day Sprint, or afterward if you need to give yourself a little time and distance. Right now, it may seem like a pretty straightforward process—you just look at what's working and what's not. But in reality, evaluating is likely to feel personal. Why? Because you have to face not only your fear of failure but also your fear of *being* a failure.

Most "habit fails" actually stop at the do step. People make their apparent lack of follow-through or consistency mean something about who they are. That self-blaming leads to stopping. But, it also leads to another cycle, one of identifying as a failure. (More on this in Chapter 11.)

Instead, what if habit fails were an opportunity to get objective, evaluate what is working and what is not, and use that information to tweak the habit plan moving forward? This *is* what it looks like to be a "habit person." Just like a good writer is actually a good editor—someone willing to revisit and alter their work over and over until they get it right—a good habit person is a good tweaker. Your missteps inform what needs to be fixed, and that's so much more empowering (and practical) than self-blaming and stopping.

If you fail at a habit, it's not you—it's the habit plan.

Tweak the Plan

So after evaluating, the first thing to tweak is your WTA. Ask yourself, is my *WHEN* (my preexisting habit) practical? Does it happen consistently? Is there a different *WHEN* that's actually better to attach my new habit to?

Next, get realistic about your *THEN*. Is your new habit enough of a baseline? Do you need to make it smaller and simpler? Does it need to be a different step from perhaps a larger, more ideal routine you'd like to work up to?

Finally, get honest about your reinforcing *AFTER*. Namely, do you have one and are you doing it? Is it effective? Is it too much of its own habit and need to be simplified?

These questions are wise to consider. Likely, it'll show you some gaps in your WTA that can be resolved. But if not, you can tweak another thing: your Implementation.

Tweak the Implementation

It's time to get curious about how your Implementation went. This is no place for criticism or judgment, just honesty. Start with this question: **Did you practice your WTA?** If not, it's not too late to practice and then move into a sprint.

Other questions to consider with this phase: Did I stick to the baseline for at least the first two to three times, or did I force the ideal? Was it simply the wrong week to implement this habit? What obstacles came up—interior and exterior—that made it difficult?

Answering these questions gives you the bird's eye view you need to remove the self-blame and try, try, try again—with tweaks (and likely practicing) in hand.

Tweak the Obstacles

One other thing to consider is what to do about those obstacles you found yourself stumbling over. Think of them like a track star jumping over hurdles. How can you lower the hurdle your obstacles create, thereby making the habit easier to complete? Here are some examples:

- If you want to meditate first thing in the morning, but find yourself scrolling in bed—lower the hurdle by getting an alarm clock and charging your phone elsewhere.

- If you want to work out during naptime but the obstacle is getting in workout clothes, be like Amanda—lower the hurdle by exercising in your normal clothes. (Honestly, so many women have told me that working out in their PJs in the morning has been key to finally working out consistently.)
- If you want to plan your days each night before bed, but keep forgetting—lower the hurdle by keeping the day planner on your nightstand so it's easier to remember.

Taryn lowered the hurdle with her Taryn Time after she noticed something that prevented this habit was gathering materials for whatever activity sounded good that day. The disruption and energy it required created enough friction that she'd sometimes skip even her baseline, making consistency an issue. Taryn made this habit easier by collecting items she'd need (coloring books, cross-stitch materials, books and magazines she wanted to read, etc.) and placing them in a basket next to her desk. That way when her lunch was over, Taryn could smoothly move into Taryn Time for the day and consistently prioritize her own interests before getting back to her job.

You can work with obstacles! Consider how you can lower the hurdle to make implementing your habit easier.

If you move through the Implementation Cycle again but the habit still isn't sticking, it may be time to consider the final thing you can tweak: the habit.

Tweak the Habit

Sometimes, the habit is right but the season is wrong. Other times, you'll discover that the habit you want will only be possible if you focus on another one first. Occasionally, you need deeper help before you work on more practical habits.

When I hosted that failed Wake Up Early challenge, the personal failing on my part was largely that it was the wrong habit to begin with. Instead of forcing an early alarm (and a fuller routine to go with it), what I *really* needed to prioritize was getting to bed. Eventually doing so truly freed the way for me to finally prioritize waking up earlier.

Maybe that's the case for you?

- Perhaps you'll be able to cook dinner better if you work on meal planning first.
- It could be that if you want to exercise, you actually need an afternoon nap to have the energy to do so.
- If journaling is on your list, what you may find instead is that you need some stillness to get your thoughts together.

In the trying is the doing, and sometimes the trying shows us the actual habit we need to prioritize.

Other times, repeated failures with the same habit may just come down to it being the right habit but the wrong time. The postpartum haze comes to mind. Yes, we *need* a lot of supportive habits: time to ourselves, sleep, movement, and other soothing habits like meditation and journaling. But, it may not be the right time to prioritize it all. It's not that these habits don't matter, nor that they ultimately won't help—of course they matter, of course they'd help. But, it all just comes down to timing.

This brings us back to a key belief I introduced to you at the beginning of the SHM: habits are helpers. When you remember that habits' main job is to be supportive, you'll be able to work through the seasonal tweaks habits require, even if the tweak is to wait on a habit until a different season.

To assist you in tweaking your habit, see the Tweaking Sticky Habits Flowchart:

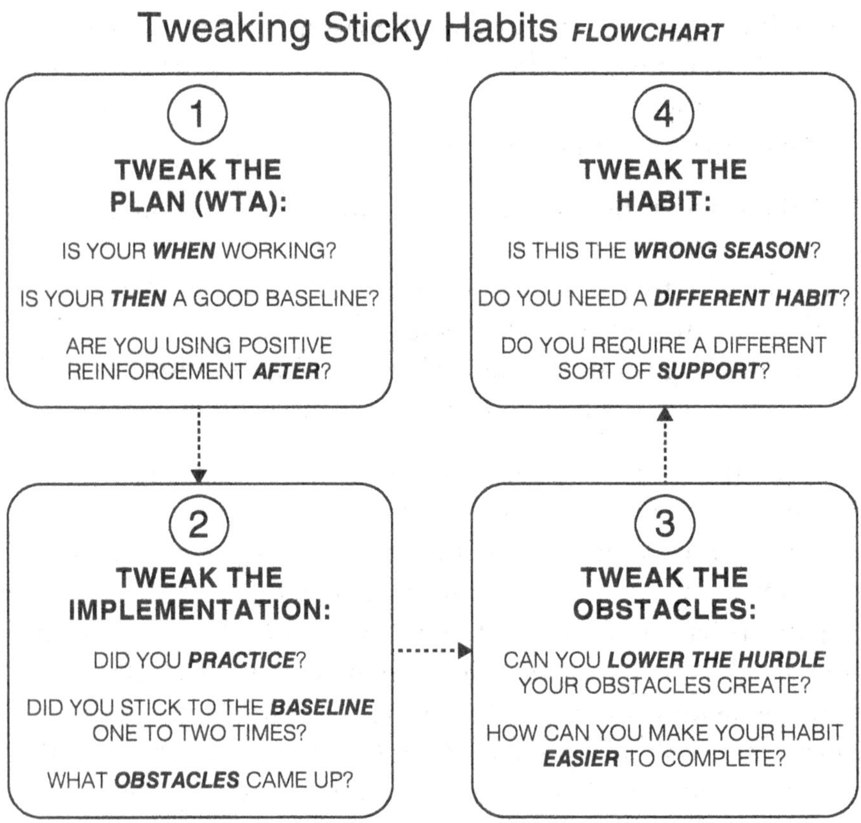

When Certain Habits Struggle

There are also deeper reasons to put off installing a habit for a season.

One client named Hilary was desperate to get her scrolling habit under control, an almost compulsive need that sucked her in more times a day than she cared to admit. There is a difference between establishing new habits and working to overcome unwanted ones, but creating a good habit or two can help make a bad habit fade into the background. We attempted to do so with

Hilary by establishing a home base for her phone and setting times of day she'd store it there so it wasn't as easy to access. To our confusion, nothing was really sticking. Instead of blaming Hilary's lack of grit, we chose to get curious about how the scrolling was serving her.

This may be confusing to hear but similar to good habits, bad habits are "helpers in disguise." Yes, they carry consequences that are ultimately *not* helping us. But in some vital ways, bad habits stick around because to a certain extent they are, in fact, "helping." I will teach you way more on this in Part Five, but Hilary's phone problem is the perfect example.

I asked Hilary, "How is scrolling actually *helping* you?" After pausing to think it through, she looked at me through the computer screen, and said in a choked-up voice,

> *"It helps me cope with my inadequacies as a mom. My mom wasn't a great source of comfort—she could actually be a source of harm. Each day, I'm trying to undo the patterns my mom instilled in me. I know I'm a good mom, but the effort to do that for my kids comes at a high cost to me internally. I feel like I'm getting dysregulated all day by the same things that would trigger my mom into a rage. I'm holding it together on the outside, but my phone is like a little release valve from all the built-up overwhelm, overstimulation, and pressure so I don't totally lose it 20 times a day on the outside."*

No wonder. Of course Hilary was resorting to a numbing behavior in ways that felt out of control. It was because her life felt out of control. With that knowledge in hand, we did two things for Hilary: (1) help her find a great therapist to work through her lingering childhood traumas and (2) find a different habit that felt gentle and supportive to give her the strength needed to work on her healing.

Now that you've learned how to tweak, it's back to the Implementation Cycle! With your updated habit plan in hand, you can *practice, do, evaluate,* and possibly *tweak* some more. If you have to move through the cycle a few times, it's okay. You're doing things right.

SARAH

Sarah took her refined—and practiced—WTA and launched into a Four-Day Sprint. Right away, she encountered an obstacle. She thought that she'd be able to get up and move right into her bathroom to get ready, but found that she actually had to use the toilet first. It was a small thing, but she had to tweak her WTA. Now it said, "WHEN *I'm done using the toilet first thing in the morning,* THEN *I'll immediately get ready (baseline: hygiene), with a simple* AFTER *of 'That's like me!'" The next day she was supposed to continue on in her sprint, but she forgot the habit . . . After a quick check-in with me, Sarah realized she hadn't practiced the new WTA. She took a few minutes to do that later in the day and lo and behold, the next morning her body automatically moved into her new habit. A few days later, and Sarah had it—her new getting ready habit was in place! Now, it was time to build.*

TAKEAWAYS: Ready to officially install your habit? Follow the Implementation Cycle: plan, practice, do, evaluate, and tweak. Practicing is a great way to train your brain. It's okay to have to go through the cycle a few times. Your failures inform how to tweak your habit: the plan, the implementation, the obstacles, and the habit.

TAKE THOUGHT: What is something you learned or a skill set you gained thanks to practicing? How do you personally want to handle your failures with implementation?

TAKE ACTION: Practice your WTA!

NOTE: For more (printables, recommended books, complementary podcast episodes, etc.), remember to check out the free and included Sticky Habit resources, available online at https://stickyhabitsbook.com/resources:

Chapter 10

Build

Learn: The fifth pillar of the Sticky Habit Method: how to build up your habit to a bigger habit or routine by adding or maximizing

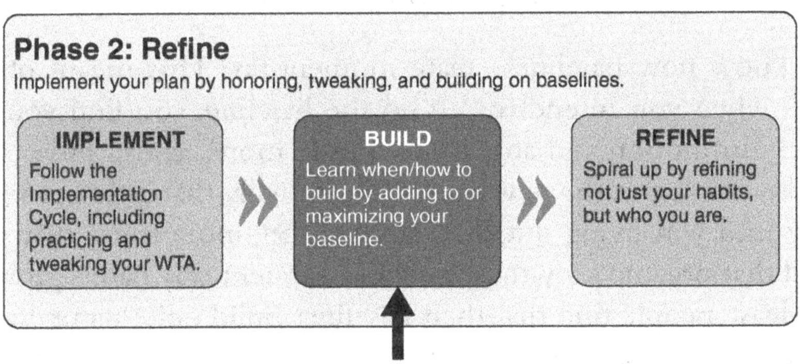

To quote the opening lines of *The Greatest Showman*, "Ladies and Gents, this is the moment you've waited for": how to take an established baseline habit and grow it more toward the ideal. I'm sure there is some annoyed part of you that wanted to learn this on day one, but here we are—actually *ready* to build. You can hate me for the delay, but I think you'll thank me for the sticky habits.

Building FAQs

Let's take this building process on, answering the most FAQs as we go.

How do you know you're ready to build?
It's simple: the baseline *feels* like a habit. It may require a little effort and a bit of remembering, but most of the time if your baseline happens fairly easily and consistently then you're ready to build. While you may want another math-inspired equation, it truly comes down to intuitively knowing you are ready.
How do you build?
Two ways: organically or intentionally.

Organically Build

You know how baselines create momentum? That means oftentimes when you intend to *just* do the baseline, you find yourself already in motion and able to do a little more. As this little more builds, it becomes the new normal. Eventually that little more will grow into you living out the ideal version, more times than not. I find that organic growth is the most frequent way habits grow. At very least, people find that their baselines build quite naturally.

If you're in the skeptical territory, why don't you try it? Go for it with your baseline habit and see how it organically builds on itself. Maybe you'll gradually hit your ideal version and on a consistent basis. Maybe your baseline grows into a bigger one, even if your ideal still isn't the norm. Regardless, you've naturally built up to something. And from there—or starting there, if you don't find things organically built up to your goal—you will be ready to head down the intentional path.

Intentionally Build

You'll know you are ready to intentionally build if you can checkmark this criteria: your baseline is consistent and you're ready for more, and (optional) you've organically built up your baseline to a certain point but feel like you've plateaued.

Intentionally building your habit toward the ideal comes in two forms, and both take me back to my limited high school math knowledge: *adding* and *multiplying*.

⊕ Adding ⊕

If your habit is part of a fuller routine that you really desire to build up to——morning, evening, getting ready, meal prep, and so on—then this is the option for you. You simply *add* on the next step (another habit!) of the routine like another link on a chain, but with a few caveats:

- This new habit must also have a baseline version.
- You begin with just that baseline, even for the first two to three times.

We are all about brain hacking, and these two caveats are vital in tricking your brain into adding on a new habit in a sustainable way. Because of this, each habit carries building potential, whether that's to do more of each part of the existing routine or to add on another habit, building up to the fuller routine.

What about the When-Then Pairing?
When adding, you still continue with the When-Then Pairing—except your original *THEN* becomes the new *WHEN* for the habit you're adding in, forming a nice habit chain.

(continued)

(continued)

Confused? I'll walk you through it using a morning routine as an example.

Imagine that ideally you'd love to wake up before your children and do a full morning routine: work out, get showered, dressed and ready, and begin making breakfast. That's three big habits stacked together into a fuller routine. You decide to start with waking up early enough to first prioritize working out, designing your baseline habit as *WHEN* I wake up to my alarm, *THEN* I'll do 10 minutes of yoga, *AFTER* I'll say "That's like me!" Thanks to that baseline, you now have that habit more times than not. You are ready to build!

Perhaps the 10-minute workout has been so simple and so easy that you're now interested in also getting ready before the kids get up. You create a new baseline habit, *adding* to your original WTA to look like this: "*WHEN* I wake up to my alarm, *THEN* I'll do 10 minutes of yoga. *WHEN* I finish yoga, *THEN* I'll rinse off in the shower and put on clean clothes. *AFTER* I'll say 'That's like me!'"

Important Notes on Adding

Using this same example, there's a few things I need to highlight that will translate to any habit you want to build by addition.

First, this growing routine still has baseline versions for each habit. If you do more than 10 minutes of yoga—whether that's a few minutes to an hour, that's great! Just remember to train your brain by sticking with the baseline version at the beginning of adding on your new getting ready habit.

Second, you may wonder if you should do *AFTER* with each step of this longer habit chain. It's up to you. If you find yourself on shaky ground or you're simply in the habit of doing so, it doesn't hurt to apply some positive reinforcement after each step as long as it requires very little effort. Remember, the *AFTER* is meant to fall off with time, so I'd just be certain to apply it after the newest habit in the chain until it indeed feels like a habit.

Third, you may notice that adding toward a morning routine will only be possible if you are inching back your bedtime as well. It brings up the question, ***Can you work on more than one habit at once?*** I'll talk about this more in the FAQ section after Chapter 11, but the quick answer is, absolutely.

As long as the new habits follow the maxims you adopted for yourself (supportive, small, simple, specific) and utilize the strategy you learned (*WHEN* + *THEN* + *AFTER*; WTA) then you can work on a few habits at once. With this example, I'd imagine the woman working on a night routine that helps her gradually get to bed earlier, simultaneously making her ideal earlier wake time more and more possible.

Adding in a new habit creates a longer habit chain, building up to the ideal routine—one that many people initially might have mistaken as a habit but then failed to keep. Instead, building via addition will not only create a routine that is longer than the first link but it'll also be thicker and stronger, too, so much so that maintaining the full routine will feel like a habit indeed.

⊗ Multiplying ⊗

If you like the habit you are on and want *more* of it, this is the option for you.

With multiplying, you focus on strengthening one habit by doing *more* of it. When your habit builds organically, it's actually by multiplying, but this can become an intentional tool when you don't see your habit building on its own.

(continued)

(continued)

If we consider the morning routine referenced in the last section, what if more than anything you know you want a longer, more effective workout? Then, you would intentionally multiply. Occasionally hitting 15 minutes of yoga is great and all, but you want to do a minimum of 30 active minutes. You decide to focus on the movement habit from your larger morning routine, multiplying how long you're exercising in five-minute increments, progressively working up toward your ideal amount.

When you multiply, you still have options on how to do so. Either you do a little more of the habit (like three more cat-cow poses) or, like the previous example, you spend a little more time doing it, building up gradually. Regardless of *how*, I'd be careful to not skip straight to making the ideal the new standard. Ideals will actually be more sustainable when they're built up to, and honestly, many women get to that point even faster than they thought they would.

Can you both add to a habit and multiply it at the same time?
Yes, you can. I'd proceed carefully, especially as you're implementing the Sticky Habit Method (SHM) for the first few times. Perhaps you can multiply the original baseline while adding in the new habit for a fuller routine.

With our morning routine gal, that can look like her multiplying her movement time to five additional minutes while also adding in a quick rinse off in the shower for her getting ready habit, both part of her longer morning routine.

Whether you're intentionally adding and/or multiplying, you should do so intuitively. This is your opportunity to learn to listen to yourself, to take stock of what you want and need, and to trust that you'll be able to know how to build. If you're not there yet, take heart—it's also your opportunity to become that curious habit scientist, willing to try and fail, then tweak and try again. Remember, a habit not sticking is a failure of the habit plan, not the person—and that tracks for building up a habit or a routine, too.

Sally Down the Street: Build

To help illustrate how to build, I want to return to Sally Down the Street and how she could possibly grow her habits. I'll first refresh your memory of her habit plan (WTA), and then provide the potential building plans with the options + for adding, and × for multiplying.

EXERCISE: Walking in morning, with a baseline of a walk around the block.

WHEN I return from dropping the kids off at school,
\+ *THEN* I will go for a walk around the block,
\+ *AFTER* I will say, "That's like me!"

  + Do five stretches (if she wants a fuller workout routine with more variety).
  × Walk around two blocks (if she wants more walking).

SPIRITUAL PRACTICE: Meditation in early afternoon, with a baseline of one minute of breathing.

WHEN I finish loading the dishwasher after lunch,
\+ *THEN* I will do one minute of deep breathing,
\+ *AFTER* I will add to my habit tracker.

(continued)

(continued)

+ Read one page of spiritual text (if she wants to read as part of her practice).
× Do three minutes of deep breathing with a mantra (if she wants more meditation).

JOURNALING: Writing in journal at night, with the baseline of one line

WHEN I finish brushing my teeth at arrive at my bed,
+ *THEN* I will write one line in my journal,
+ *AFTER* I will light my favorite candle as a reward while I read what I wrote.

+ Meditate for one minute (if she wants a full reflection/grounding routine).
× Write one paragraph (if she wants more journaling).

What about your original baseline?

Your baselines build. So, what used to be your "worst day baseline" may now happen so occasionally that you notice you actually have a new and bigger baseline that you can hit more times than not. Yay!

Even then, you still have your OG baseline. (I know I'm not cool enough to pull off using the *Original Gangster* phrase, but just go with it. We millennials think *OG* stands for *original*.)

You can keep your OG baselines tucked in your pocket for when there's a seasonal shift (literal or figurative) that reduces your energy levels or changes your circumstances, making your go-to built-up habits and routines harder to stick with. That original baseline can help you stay on the consistency wagon, or get back on it if you had a forced pause.

I find myself going back to my OG baselines whenever my kids transition from being at school to being at home (holidays, summer) or vice versa (back to school). This shift requires huge internal and external changes for all of us. I know that in order to be my best self and help my kids adjust, I need to be supported by my own keystone habits. However, forcing the ideals I built up to would honestly come at too high a cost—whether that's in time or attitude. (Ask me how grumpy I was at the beginning of the last summer break thanks to not being flexible with my habits.) When I'm wise in these seasons, my OGs are there to catch me.

I also love my OGs when I face a period of high stress (let's say when a manuscript is due—not speaking from experience or anything), or if I find myself in a mental health slump, or I feel a bout of burnout coming on. This built-in gentleness still gives me the support I need without the ball and chain.

Finally, even your OGs (okay I'll stop referring to them that way now) are allowed to change or to be paused.

- If you break your leg, it would be stupid to go on a walk around the block for exercise.
- If little league baseball season has ruined any semblance of an evening routine, maybe you hit pause on your nightly wind-down ritual until your kid's team inevitably falls out of the tournament, because you raised participants not winners.

Remember, you can do the same habit in different ways! You aren't stuck working out, journaling, meal prepping, meditating, and getting ready the same way the rest of your life. If a baseline of a habit you love and need doesn't work for a particular season, do it in a different way and create a new baseline to go with it.

Flexibility makes consistency possible not just day to day, but year to year. Being the habit person you (now) are means you know that you are playing the ultimate long game. Being both supple and intuitive with your habits is how you can maintain them for a lifetime, or even for the season you need them to be in. This is one of the roots of why the SHM is different—it's about you *trusting* yourself. With time, you learn that you do in fact know what is best for you and that you can believe and depend on yourself, too.

While you're learning that trust, you can reference the Building Sticky Habits flowchart here:

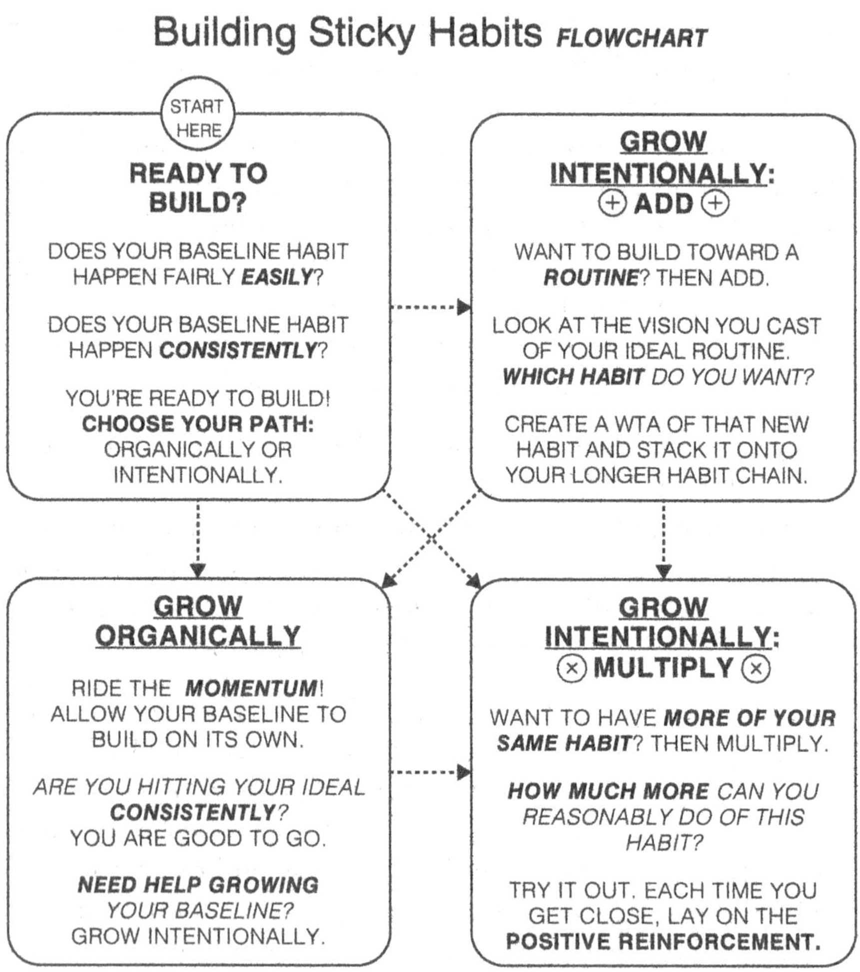

SARAH

Sarah was feeling both more confident and able to build thanks to having a solid get-ready habit in place. More days than not, Sarah was able to hit her hygiene baseline, but the original reason this habit mattered to her was the desire to express herself. Clean teeth can only go so far! That insight pushed Sarah to maximize what she had in place by doing more to get ready for the day. But, Sarah felt a little stuck because there were almost too many options beyond her hygiene baseline: getting dressed in a cute outfit, doing her hair, getting make up on, and even layering on accessories. As fun as it all sounded, doing everything took time and energy Sarah couldn't consistently expect for now and she worried she would set herself up to fail. So, how should she maximize?

To answer this, I took Sarah back to her why *behind selecting this habit: she wanted to feel like herself. "Sarah," I prompted her, "out of all those other getting ready options, which one would help you feel like* you *the most?" She surprised us both by choosing accessories. "Monica, I can wear the most basic outfit, have my hair in a ponytail, and not a stitch of makeup on, but feel so much more like my cute self when I have a fun pair of earrings on." We had our answer! The intentional way for Sarah to build was to accessorize. The other steps could come with time, whether intentionally or organically, but if all she could do for a bit was hygiene and earrings, she was one step closer to feeling more like herself than she had in years, and empowered to take on her day with darling earrings swinging alongside her.*

Sarah chose to maximize her getting ready habit. How do you want to build your own habit: adding or multiplying? Regardless of what you choose, you know the way.

TAKEAWAYS: You know you're ready to build a habit when your baseline happens easily and consistently. While much of building happens organically, you can do so intentionally as well by adding or multiplying. Adding is tacking on the next habit of an ideal routine. You still need a baseline and a WTA for this new habit. Multiplying is doing more of the habit you already have, building up to a truer ideal. Baselines build, too, but your original baselines will always be there. Trust yourself to know what you need, and build from there.

TAKE THOUGHT: Which kind of building appeals the most to you right now: adding or multiplying? If you are adding, what is your new WTA?

TAKE ACTION: Look at the Building Habits Flowchart to sort out which path is right for you.

NOTE: For more (printables, recommended books, complementary podcast episodes, etc.), remember to check out the free and included Sticky Habit resources, available online at https://stickyhabitsbook.com/resources:

Chapter 11

Refine

Learn: The sixth (and final!) pillar of the Sticky Habit Method: how to Refine not just your habits, but who you are

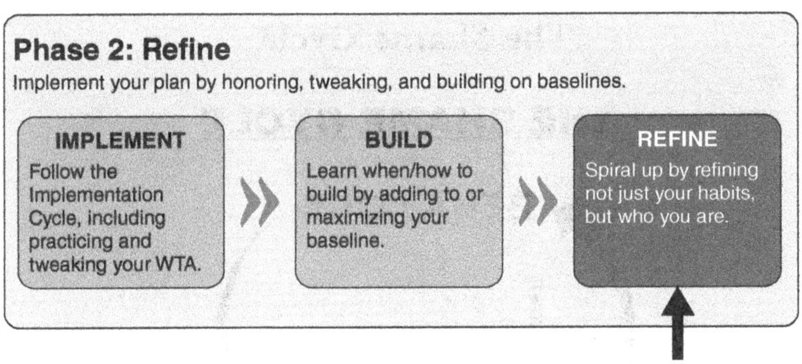

As you move through the Implementation Cycle with one habit after the next, you're not just refining your habits, *you are refining who you are.* That's right—habits go deeper.

In Chapter 8, I introduced the behavior-identity cycle. Quick refresher: the way you behave affects the way you see yourself, and the way you see yourself shapes the way you behave.

This cycle can be used for bad or for good. Are you ready to officially learn how?

You likely are already well familiar with the bad version, because you've been living it out in one way or another. Shame often drives and increases behaviors that "prove" the worst parts of yourself as *who* you are. This is how the pattern becomes the Shame Cycle.

The Shame Cycle

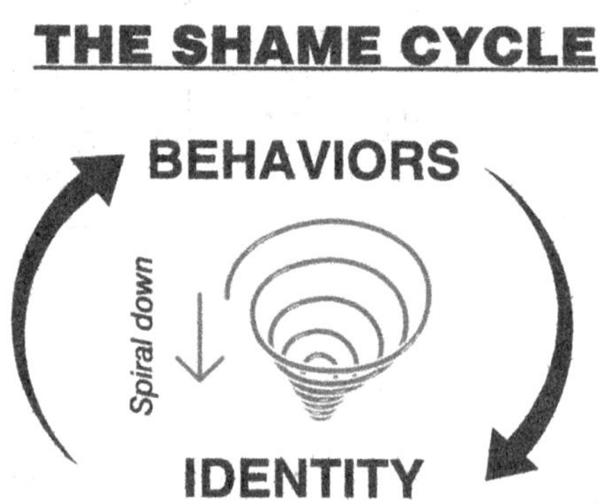

When your actions are "bad" (e.g., yelling at your kids, not following through with an intention), they form beliefs about who you think you are—aka, your identity. Then, the way you see yourself almost inevitably leads to more behaviors that match that identity. Shame drives this pattern until it becomes a cycle that spirals down, getting tighter and tighter as it goes until there's almost no space between thoughts and behaviors.

I often see this play out with neurodiverse kids who deal with a great deal of internalized shame. Several of my children are neurodiverse, almost all with ADHD—and each a different manifestation of it. (Silver lining: parenting is rarely boring!) During a rough season when one child had an especially hard time controlling his impulses, he screamed back to my attempts at redirection, "I'm just a bad kid. I'm bad, bad, bad!" These weren't things I had told him about himself, but he knew how he was being perceived at school, at church, and occasionally (I'm sorry to admit) at home. This self-image seemed to constantly be confirmed by the evidence around him, and the shame of it all only perpetuated the cycle, making it really hard to interrupt.

Shame as a Self-Fulfilling Prophesy

What are some shame-driven labels you've assigned yourself? How do you see evidence in your behaviors that supports that image?

Maybe some of these broader labels match both your thoughts and your actions:

- I am lazy.
- I lack follow-through.
- I am weak.
- I don't have self-control.
- I am all-or-nothing.
- I don't have what it takes.
- I can't self-motivate.
- I am not disciplined.

How has your conviction that you are "bad at habits" created behaviors that serve as evidence for that belief?

Shame is sneaky. You may think that in order to change you must be hyper-diligent (read: harsh) with yourself. You treat yourself just like I did as a first-year teacher, catching every sign of weakness and misstep right in the moment and dishing out immediate, stern consequences. The thing is, shame doesn't just feel bad—it's ineffective at sustainable behavior change.

Shame's Antidote: Self-Compassion

In her book, *Self-Compassion*, psychologist, researcher, and writer Kristin Neff explores how turning inward with kindness, grace, and encouragement to oneself is a marker for the resilience it takes to *truly* and deeply change. Self-compassion's opposite is shame, which Neff deems as destructive thanks to its penchant for extreme self-criticism and hiding imperfection from others. With shame, people stay stuck in the mire instead of working through it. Neff teaches that self-compassion is the antidote to shame. We can use kindness instead of judgment to identify our faults and failures, then do something about them while accepting that we are allowed to be human.[1]

Brené Brown's research differentiates guilt ("I did something bad") from shame as an identity-driver ("I *am* bad"). Brown has devoted her life's work as a researcher and writer to shame, perfectionism, and the power of connection. In her book, *The Gifts of Imperfection*, Brown describes shame as an "intensely painful feeling or experience of believing we are flawed and therefore unworthy of love, belonging, and connection."[2]

[1] Kristin Neff, *Self-Compassion: The Proven Power of Being Kind to Yourself* (William Morrow, 2011).

[2] Brené Brown, *The Gifts of Imperfection,* 10th anniv. ed. (Hazelden, 2022).

Does that description sound like someone who can pick themselves up and change in good and sustainable ways? Obviously not. And yet, I get the worry that accepting shortcomings must surely lead to apathy. That simply isn't true. Neff and Brown often combine their research on shame with original research done by June Tangney and Ronda Dearing. In their book, *Shame and Guilt*, Tangney and Dearing teach, "Shame motivates a desire to hide, disappear, or escape." These avoidant behaviors inhibit growth, not encourage it.[3]

By contrast, self-compassion allows for guilt to be separate from identity, encouraging change from a place of acceptance and compassion. Carl Rogers, one of the fathers of modern psychology, taught this truth over and over again: **"The curious paradox is that when I accept myself, just as I am, then I can change"** [emphasis added].[4] Acceptance does not equate apathy.

Self-compassion isn't about becoming a Pollyanna, one who is endlessly optimistic and perhaps naively disconnected from reality. You're allowed to be human. You can acknowledge the hard moments, the mistakes you made, the valid feelings you have that may not always be good and positive.

Self-compassion isn't about lying to yourself. Instead, think of compassion as the way you'd talk to a friend or to a child who needs to master a new skill, overcome a tendency, or improve a situation. You'd tell them the truth—and gently so—while also celebrating every sign that they're moving in the right direction. This kind of compassion is what will give you the patience you need to persist, and to do so well, because true change takes time.

What does this all mean? It means to change in the ways you want, you need to be kind to yourself. You need to practice self-compassion. And yes, I mean "practice" as learning to do so will

---

[3] June Price Tangney and Ronda L. Dearing, *Shame and Guilt (Emotions and Social Behavior)* (Guilford Press, 2002).

[4] Carl Rogers, *On Being a Person: A Therapist's View of Psychotherapy* (Houghton Mifflin Harcourt, 1961).

necessitate the same persistent effort as learning an instrument. It will require consistent work to unwind the long-standing shame-driven patterns of self-criticism, comparison, isolation, harshness, and self-abandonment. I can tell you from experience that you will grow exponentially more with self-compassion as the inner driver, not shame.

Shift from Spiraling Down to Spiraling Up

As yucky as it is to identify the Shame Cycle, it's the first step to deep and practical change. Just as you can spiral down, you can also spiral up! And you do so in two ways:

- Interrupt the Shame Cycle.
- Lean into the Progress Cycle.

To interrupt the Shame Cycle, you stop mid-cycle between Behavior and Identity and refuse to affirm your missteps as evidence of *who* you are. It really comes down to spotting the connection with thoughts and behaviors. This requires a level of awareness that will feel foreign at first, but will get easier over time.

Awareness is half the battle to all change.

I find it helps to see these shameful thoughts as a person separate from yourself—an outsider and harsh critic that takes up residence in your head, just like the trolls from the internet do on your feeds. Sadly, this voice is sometimes directly tied to a parent or another loved one from your past or even present. (Those childhood experiences and attachments run deep.) Removing this shame voice from *who you are* is so powerful. It not only helps you notice the absurdity of what that voice is telling you, it also empowers you to talk back to it as your compassionate self.

Rebecca (of the five-minute walk fame) and I got a kick out of the nickname she applied to her inner critic voice—Sharon—a combination of Shame and Karen. In this phase of awareness, I'd hear from her, "Monica, Sharon got sneaky with me today! Here's what she said . . . ." "So, Sharon is talking smack today! I told her to take a break." We would chuckle at Sharon, then replace her with a nurturing voice.

Let's say you've always wanted to be an early bird, but have found it near impossible to get into the habit. Here's how stopping the Shame Cycle could look on a day when you, once again, wake up later than intended.

Pre-interrupting the Shame Cycle:

★You wake up and see the late time.★

"Oh, no! I did it again. I'm the worst. I have no self-discipline."

You jump out of bed and rush to get ready, grumbling and guilting yourself all the while.

Post-interrupting the Shame Cycle:

★You wake up and see the late time.★

"Oh, no! I did it again. I'm the worst. I have no self-discipline."

>> AWARENESS KICKS IN <<

"Ah, there's that harsh voice. Yes, it's true—I didn't wake up when I intended to, but it doesn't mean I have no discipline. I want to be better, and it's time to get more clarity on why this habit is so hard for me. It's okay, I will figure this out."

You jump out of bed, refusing to let the voice ruin the rest of your morning.

Interrupting the Shame Cycle is vital to reject not just the bad behaviors but a bad self-image. It helps you stop spiraling down and start spiraling up. It won't be perfect, or even easy, but it will be possible as you lean into the Progress Cycle.

The Progress Cycle

Whenever your behaviors align with *who you want to be* (note: not who the shame voice *tells* you who are), affirm any beliefs about yourself that back up those behaviors. That identity—the self-image that Bassham discovered as key for performance—must be reinforced: the more the better.

Awareness is again key to this version of the cycle. *Any* time you notice an action that acts as evidence of the self-image you desire, you've got to call it out like a toddler successfully using the potty. And it can be those three simple words Bassham was so fond of: "That's like me!"

It can also be things like, "I did it!" "Look at me—this is who I am." "Wow, I am a ____ [fill in the blank with the desired identity]."

Regardless of what you say, that positive affirmation not only affirms both behaviors and identities, it also *confirms* them in you. The more you affirm, the tighter and more concrete both sides of the Progress Cycle become. As you spiral up, it gets easier and easier to do, until you don't even really have to think about it—it's just *who you are*.

It may help to apply this cycle to the wanna-be early-bird example referenced previously.

You've been working on building awareness of the shame voice while also establishing a baseline habit that helps you get up earlier, a little bit at a time. It's just your first week, so your earlier wake time is five minutes sooner than normal. The alarm goes off, you stop it, but before you get out of bed you take a moment to feel some pride. You say to yourself, "That's like me! I'm an early riser." Now, with some boosted confidence backing you, you're ready to face the day.

Replacing Sharon

If this all still feels foreign to you, just know that it did to my client, Rebecca, too! Her Sharon voice was not only strong—it was the default. Rebecca said to me, "You are the first person in my life who told me I didn't have to be forceful with myself in order to change." The first several months of our coaching were about Rebecca's *loud* inner critic. She was truly convinced of its efficacy, until we were able to uncover how her years of self-help obsession were hurting more than helping. The shame was driving her tendency to be harsh with herself, to not trust herself, and to beat herself up with other people's prescriptions, leading her to crash and burn. It was a pattern she didn't know how to get out of.

When I taught her the Shame and Progress Cycles and explained how self-compassion is the antidote to shame, Rebecca visibly balked. Wouldn't being kinder to herself just give her permission to rest on her laurels, say "take me or leave me" to herself and others, and not try anymore? No, actually. Because empathy drives wise action, the kind that can stick around.

With a little doubt lingering but enough courage to override it, Rebecca chose to change in a new way: one driven by self-compassion. We had to work *hard* on Rebecca's awareness of Sharon's voice in her head, and to use her experienced teacher voice to talk back to Sharon in a wise and kind, but firm way. Over many months, the noticing and the talking back became more and more natural, until Rebecca found her true, real voice became more of the default. And what do you know? The habits she had long been working and failing at—from fitness to home systems—were working better than ever.

Rebecca stunned me at the beginning of one of our final calls with the first words out of her mouth, "I'm really proud of me." Perhaps that doesn't feel like a shocking statement, but from Rebecca it was. I asked her to tell me more and she explained about how the transition from summer to back-to-school was disrupting the habits she had worked hard to install. But, instead of getting mad at herself and thereby crashing and burning, she inserted self-compassion. She accepted that a seasonal shift will require shifting habits, she tracked how she could adapt them, and do so in ways that were more of a gentle push than an all-or-nothing whip.

Rebecca said, "Before, it felt wrong to believe that I could be kind to myself and still change. But now, there's a layer of confidence in me that wasn't there before." Thanks to anchoring into a kind voice and the Progress Cycle, Rebecca trusted herself. She believed that she could do it, that she could change and keep changing, that she was the person she always longed to be.

Messy, Wide Arcs of Change

What if self-acceptance was the key to healing? What if kindness drove the changes you so desire? What if working on your habits isn't just about what you *do*, it's about who you *are*? It's time to test these what-if's out.

While in the Progress Cycle, you are spiraling up. This doesn't mean a straight upshoot—it means there will be messy, wide arcs and lessons that have to be revisited time and time again. When you commit to a lifetime of spiraling up, you accept you won't get it right every time. You know that as long as you're facing the right direction and you're trying, you're doing it right.

To help you do so, I want to briefly introduce you to my three Characteristics of Change, values that are vital to a life of staying in the Progress Cycle.

Three Characteristics of Change—values for lifelong growth:

- Compassion
- Curiosity
- Courage

Compassion

I already broke down the importance of compassion, so I'll mention just a few things to drive it home.

First, here are some synonyms of compassion that may resonate with you more deeply: acceptance, empathy, and grace. Carl Jung, a 20th-century pioneer in psychology, said this, "We cannot change anything until we accept it. Condemnation does not liberate, it oppresses."[5] Like Rebecca and so many other women who have had to reframe the way they drive their progress, you will come to learn that true and lasting change comes from compassion.

If there's one thing I've learned in coaching hundreds of women, it's this root we share as humans: the desire to improve, and the worry that it's just not possible for us.

Shame is the fear that we can't change. Compassion is the faith that we absolutely can.

[5] Carl G. Jung, *Modern Man in Search of a Soul* (Harcourt, Brace & World, 1933/1953).

This is the kind of faith I'm asking you to own for yourself, the kind that you can only gain by taking a giant leap into the dark and trusting that something will be there to catch you on the other side. Spoiler: it'll be *someone*, and it'll be *you*.

Curiosity

Thanks to the messy, wide arcs of change, you will experience failure. (Sound familiar?) To move through failure differently and more productively requires a willingness to be curious.

Whereas the inner critic wants you to dissect the many ways *you* are a failure, curiosity detaches your self-worth from the outcome and objectively takes stock of what happened. I call this the *zoom out*, when you take on a bird's eye view of a situation and dissect it as if it were someone else. When you zoom out, you can *see* the facts: what circumstances contributed to the failure, what unexpected obstacles came up, how internal resistance played a part, and anything else that might be getting in your way. Those details inform what you can tweak and how you can stay in the Progress Cycle.

If you need a little help in the curiosity department, try out my WIN-WIN formula. I use it personally and with my clients when they're feeling a little stuck in getting objective. The WIN-WIN formula is an acronym with three steps for you to follow, two for the first *win* (spelled "WN," sorry if that's confusing, just pretend you're a teenager in the early aughts and don't believe in vowels!), and one question for the second *win* (spelled normally!):

WIN-WIN FORMULA

W: What went WELL?
N: What did NOT?

W: WHAT's
I: IMPORTANT
N: NOW?

Answering those questions as objectively (and compassionately) as possible is what helps you piece together the information you need to tweak and to try again. It's a formula you can use to get curious when doing so feels tricky.

When Taryn of the Taryn Time example experienced a shift to her work schedule, she found herself also having to reexamine those afternoon self-care sessions. Once she made the switch, she found herself forgetting about Taryn Time completely. During our coaching call, I could sense some sheepishness as she explained needing my help. She expressed being embarrassed that she had to "start all over" after having this habit for some time.

Before we proceeded to troubleshoot, I asked Taryn to answer my curiosity-based questions. (PS. Taryn came up with the WIN-WIN acronym afterward! I'm forever grateful.)

What went WELL?

"After not having it for a few weeks, I can see that this habit supports me even more than I originally thought. It's nice to know it makes a difference. Also, I'm here and requesting help instead of blaming myself for falling off the wagon. I'm proud of myself for that!"

What did NOT?

"I can see now that when my work schedule changed, I didn't account for how that would affect this time of day. I forgot to strategize a new When-Then Pairing, so my habit slipped away."

What's Important Now?

"I need to strategize how to keep this habit going with a WTA [WHEN + THEN + AFTER] *for Taryn Time that matches my current reality."*

Thanks to this boost in curiosity, Taryn was able to also insert more compassion and later curiosity as we crafted a new WTA for this old habit.

If I could only choose one thing my most successful clients have had in common—the women who overcame odds, persevered, and made dramatic progress—it was the characteristic of curiosity. Without it, the other two are a lot harder to come by.

Courage

It weirdly requires a great deal of courage to believe in the process of change: small wins build over time. Doing so asks you to go outside the norm, to say no to all-or-nothing thinking, to pursue the same goals in different ways, to believe in the long game, and to own your capacity to truly, deeply change. You know what I just described? A Revolutionizer.

Adopt what one of my first clients said, as noted in Chapter 5: "It takes the greatest of courage to do the smallest of things."

Remember, you are a Revolutionizer. You dare to do things differently. However, to change big things and in big ways, you have to start small and you have to start with yourself. Bigger shifts will come with time, from transforming how you handle big emotions, to changing whole-family systems. But first, you need to embody that "greatest of courage" and start with one small habit that will help you feel more like yourself.

SARAH

Sarah told me something profound in one of our later coaching calls. "Monica, I feel like everything I've learned and worked on with you is coming together to not just help my life, but change it deeply. I feel so much more like me, and not because I had to, but because I chose to. I feel empowered to continue on this trajectory because I not only know the way, I believe and know myself and that I can do this."

What started as a simple hygiene-only baseline grew to so much more, and it wasn't just that now Sarah was getting more fully ready for the day more times than not. This simple habit inspired Sarah to work on prioritizing other areas of her life both externally (like setting up her new art room) and internally (like her bad habit of emotionally eating to numb out negative feelings). At the root of it all, Sarah didn't worry as much. Thanks to her growing understanding that sustainable change takes time, Sarah knew she could change—and she knew how.

TAKEAWAYS: As you refine your habits, you also refine *who* you are. While the Shame Cycle leads you to stay stuck in the worst ways you see yourself, the Progress Cycle helps you spiral up both in behavior and in identity. Notice the inner voice and how it speaks to you. Seek to affirm the good and be real about the bad. Instead of shame, use compassion, curiosity, and courage to mold who you are and how you act.

TAKE THOUGHT: How have you seen *compassion* combat shame in your life, leading to progress? What is your own inner voice like?

TAKE ACTION: Practice one of the Three Characteristics of Change: compassion, curiosity, and courage.

NOTE: For more (printables, recommended books, complementary podcast episodes, etc.), remember to check out the free and included Sticky Habit resources, available online at https://stickyhabitsbook.com/resources:

A Pause to Answer Your Sticky Habit Method (SHM) FAQs

Before you learn how to revise the bad habits blocking your progress, let's pause to answer the most frequently asked questions that come up with the SHM. Feel free to browse through and only take the time to read through the questions you have, and come back to reference this section as needed.

Do I follow every step of the SHM for each habit I work on the rest of my life?

Short answer: no. You really won't have to.

I would advise following the SHM step-by-step for the first few habits that you work on using the method, specifically. Forming habits is a skill, and this method is made up of many. With those skill sets in hand (plus more confidence, too) you can use a few tools from the SHM that are particularly helpful, like having a clear WTA, starting with a baseline, or practicing the habit before game time.

You can always move through each step of the SHM whenever a habit isn't sticking or it's historically complicated for you.

The best part about doing progress differently is that you learn to trust yourself far more than when you rely on the black-and-white prescriptions of others. Living more intuitively is the main goal for each woman I work with. With time, you'll know more for yourself which parts of the SHM you need as you install a new habit, from one helpful concept to the whole kit and caboodle.

Does every part of my life need to be a habit?

When women find success with the SHM, they get really excited and can be tempted to "habitize" every area of their life.

This can be empowering at first, but I find the idea of having a regimented life to be debilitating when put in practice.

So, should cleaning out your garage every six months be a habit? Should you overhaul every need into a routine or system? Should each day be filled with one habit after the next?

No. Some things are just to-dos. In fact, I'd say most are.

The goal of being a habit person isn't to become a robot who performs each duty with exactness all day every day. The goal of being a habit person is to have a life!

Think of habits more as touchpoints to your day: moments that center and support you. Habits are there for the most important times and tasks of the day, but the rest of the time will be where you *live*. You'll cross things off your to-do list, you'll connect with your loved ones, you'll scroll social media when you need a break, you'll have hobbies, and for goodness sake you'll *rest*.

Not everything needs to be a habit.

What if I don't have the luxury of working up to a habit?

There will be times when the ideal versions of our habits have to be installed right away without the typical buildup. Whether it's a new job that forces dramatic shifts in our sleep or a child has an immediate need that requires your full support—that's life.

When those moments come, know that it's absolutely okay to go for the ideals. Just try to make those occasions rare, do your best to keep it to one habit at a time, and also acknowledge that there will be a price to pay. That price may be reflected in your energy, capacity, health, or relationships.

Acknowledging all of this gives you space to be as gentle as possible with yourself and to bolster your most important habits. Doing so provides more bandwidth to proceed in ways where the price doesn't outweigh the benefits of the desired outcome.

Finally, if you do apply an ideal right away and it doesn't stick—even if it was, in fact, one you *thought* demanded a quick install—please be compassionate with yourself. Zoom out, consider which strategies from the SHM you can use, and try again. And, yes, that may mean swallowing your pride and starting again with a baseline.

Can I work on more than one habit at a time?

As I briefly touched on in Chapter 10, yes, you absolutely can. However, I'd do so with two caveats:

- Only proceed to installing multiple habits once you're comfortable with the SHM. Doing so will ensure you have built up the skill sets and confidence you need to advance your implementation.
- Whether or not you move through each step of each phase of the SHM, ensure that the habits you install simultaneously hit the Sweet Spot of the Sticky Habit Matrix: supportive, small, simple, and specific.

Even then, I wouldn't shoot for more than two to three habits at a time if sustainability is your goal—and it should be.

When will I know if my habit is sticky?

A habit is working for you if you don't have to exert a lot of energy to remember it, doing so feels natural, and you hit it more times than not.

While there are some habits that may still require effort (day planning is that for me), as long as the other steps are in place then you can consider it sticky.

What if a habit doesn't stick?

This will happen. There is no foolproof habit implementation, no matter what the salesperson say. (And yes, I'm being sassy and salesperson equates to anyone online selling you their black-and-white method.) Expect some frustrations and even failures with every single habit you install.

When a habit doesn't stick, revisit the end of Chapter 9 and the flowchart, "Tweaking Sticky Habits."

Can I have seasonal habits?

100%! In fact, I'd go so far as to say that if you have seasonal habits, then you are doing habits right. Having a sticky habit doesn't mean it has to stick until you're 100 years old and on your deathbed.

I swam a great deal for exercise over a few years' time, but I haven't done so much as a lap since COVID-19 hit. This was not a habit fail. Swimming was something I needed in that season of my life, and now I don't. If that changes and I want to make swimming laps a regular part of my life again, I can pick it back up.

Seasonal can be figurative (a phase of life) or literal (winter, spring, etc.). Give yourself permission to let your habits flow with the season you are in and in ways that are ultimately meeting the most important purpose they serve: support. That means habits can come, they can go, or they can change, just as long as they're helping.

You can also have seasonal habits that are purely about enjoying the one you're in. Reading in front of the fire in the afternoon is my favorite habit during winter months, but I don't prioritize reading at that time during the summer, and most definitely not in front of the fire. Getting up early for a sunrise walk is a wonderful way to begin a summer day, but I honestly feel sad doing the same thing in the dark cold winter.

Your habits are meant to match your season—so let them!

Should habits always be the feel-good kind?

While "feel-good" was an essential ingredient I introduced in Chapter 6, in truth—no, you don't have to be obsessed and thrilled with a habit in order to prioritize it. As long as it really is a chosen habit—not a should—some habits' natural consequences are what feel good, so they're still worth prioritizing.

I feel this way about waking up early. To be honest, I dread it. When my alarm goes off in the very early morning hours, I despise every step of getting out of my warm bed, stumbling across the room to turn off my alarm, and moving into my cold bathroom to get dressed in my workout clothes. And yet, being an early riser is the second most important habit of my life for this season. Because of that, I still prioritize this habit. *But*, there are ways I still aspire to make it feel-good, so I hate it less and still reap the desired rewards.

I like to pair a yay! feeling with a blah task. A few ways you can pair: audio (music, audiobooks, podcasts), warm beverages, lighting a candle, and quality items that boost the appeal (like good workout clothes, a nice day planner, good sheets for the bed, etc.).

Literal rewards right after the blah habit are also great. I personally do this by gifting myself a piece of chocolate, or visiting Page

Six online (don't judge), or watching a short YouTube video as an intentional break after meeting an allotted amount of productivity.

What happens when I still want a habit, but I need it to shift?
Not to be a broken record, but this will happen and it'll be normal. Shifting a habit to match a season is especially important for the keystones in our lives.

As you may recall, sleep is my most important keystone habit, and yet I'm allowed to prioritize it differently based on my season. When my kids were really little (phase of life), I absolutely wouldn't have insisted on being an early bird. Same goes with other phases, such as when I'm struggling with sleep—whether it be insomnia or a kid who has sleep issues—or when I am ill. When the weather changes and with it school is in or out of session, I shift my sleep habits to go with those seasonal phases, whether it's moving up bed and wake times or allowing myself to not have either.

If you give yourself permission for your habits to be seasonal, then you'll be better able to go back to the basics of how to redesign this habit for right here, right now. I recommend doing so by considering these questions:

- What will make this habit supportive for this particular period?
- How do I want this habit to make me feel?
- How much time and energy am I working with now?
- What limitations do I currently have?
- What other circumstances are important to consider for this habit?

Your answers will give you all you need to know to create a new habit plan (WTA) and try it on for size. If it doesn't work, then tweak and try again, trusting that you *will* get there, because you will!

What if a bad habit is acting as the main obstacle to installing a good one?
Then it's time for you to read through Part Five . . . and, as you likely guessed, this is totally normal and to be expected.

Part Five

REVISE: APPLY THE STICKY HABIT METHOD TO FIX YOUR BAD HABITS

Habit Story 4

Name: Jill

Responsibilities: Full-time special education teacher nearing retirement, married with two adult children and one grandchild; Jill's adult son is a person with autism[1]

Habit fail: Time to self? Regulation?

Jill didn't know quite when it started, just that it was her go-to way of dealing with the stress of her work: mindless munching. It didn't necessarily feel like full-blown, out-of-control binging, but it still felt like a problem. She would find herself eating snacks or candy in stolen moments of downtime throughout her busy day as a special ed teacher. Jill prioritized wellness and nutrition, so it felt out of character for her to get sucked into what many would describe as emotional eating. And the consequences weren't great. It wasn't even about weight, although that was a small factor. Jill's stomach often felt upset, she lacked energy thanks to having more sugar than nutrition, and she didn't feel hungry for her actual lunch so she often skipped it or felt overfull when she got to it. Consequently, Jill worried whether she was setting herself up to age well with retirement quickly approaching. But, no matter how often she told herself she wasn't going to get sucked into mindless munching while working that day, she still somehow gravitated to this bad habit. Jill felt ashamed that for someone who did so much so well, she couldn't fix this bad habit.

[1]Members of the autism community have different preferences on how they would like autism to be addressed using either person-first or diagnosis-first language. Person-first is how Jill prefers to refer to her son's special needs.

Numbing out is something we all do as humans. From scrolling our phones to emotional eating, bad habits are annoying at best, and destructive at worst. But, what if these habits were actually trying to help? What if we changed how we looked at our numbing-out behaviors, and by extension, ourselves? What if instead of erasing bad habits from our lives we tried to work *with* them? Part Five will teach you to use principles from the Sticky Habit Method to do what you may have wanted to start with all along: *revise* bad habits.

Before we proceed, I want to give both a disclaimer and a trigger warning: Jill joined one-on-one coaching with me to help her make decisions about her career, mainly if and when to retire and how to do so smoothly. Her habit of emotional eating was something that came along for the ride, as habits often do with each of my clients. We approached this habit with great care, starting with me getting assurance that what Jill described as a "bad habit" wasn't in fact disordered eating. With her honest answers and understanding of the behaviors, she and I both felt confident her mindless munching was more in the territory of a self-soothing habit that happened strictly at work, but not to the level of it being an addiction or a disorder. If at any point it felt more serious than that, both Jill and I knew that the next step for her was to work with a therapist that was certified in disordered eating and/or eating disorders. Fortunately, that wasn't needed. But, that's not true for everybody.

Addictions and disorders often start with what looks like "bad habits." They can stay in that territory, but what makes them worse is the compulsiveness of those behaviors, the consequences of them, and the full body-and-mind control they hold over those suffering from them. Only you can know when habits become something more, so tread with caution through the next part. And if you realize that something you thought was a "bad habit" is actually much more, please seek out professional support. I did when I was 20 years old, and I'm grateful for that every single day. You can find therapists in your area on *Psychology Today*'s website.

You can sort by your insurance or what area of your life you are wanting to work on.

Finally, while the chapters under Part Five won't technically be about an eating disorder or disordered eating, the eating nature of the behavior Jill and I worked on may trigger those who are dealing with disordered behaviors concerning food. Proceed through her story with care, which will always be separated, named, and italicized.

Chapter 12

A Different Way to View and Change Bad Habits

Learn: What bad habits are, why they stick, and the steps to revise them

I hated it. I felt ashamed of it. I kept the extent of it from my husband. And I wondered why I did it when it went against who I thought I was as a person: online shopping.

I was raised in an extremely frugal home. With seven children under one roof, I am sure keeping us all fed, clothed, and active with our interests was a constant stress for both of my parents. They managed that stress well, and largely by being extremely thrifty. I easily followed suit by squirreling away my literal pennies from the earliest memories I can recall, using a special piggy bank my mom gave me with three categories: donate, spend, and save. I was naturally a saver and truly didn't have a difficult time holding onto my hard-earned funds from my neighborhood babysitting jobs and later my real jobs as a teen and young adult. I was proud of my growing bank account and the wise choices I made in how I used my money.

So, my bad habit of online shopping as a young stay-at-home mom came as a surprise to me.

It started with good intentions, as most things do. I found myself frequenting T.J. Maxx, seeking affordable ways to clothe my growing family and outfit our small home. But my visits grew more frequent, and with screaming young shoppers in my cart, my purchases became more frenetic and less thoughtful. I found myself getting more than we needed, then coming home and feeling terrible about the full bags. I'd head back to T.J. Maxx to make returns, but would circle the aisles "real quick" on our way out, only to move through the whole cycle once again.

In my pursuit to get a better hold on this bad habit, I swore off frequenting my once favored budget store, à la "stay out of the bar." Then, I got my first iPhone right around when I had my third baby. Nursing sessions turned into scrolling sessions at odd moments day and night as I perused the latest deals. My thrifty values felt like they were setting me up to fail as I chased sale after sale, then return after return. The momentary rush of getting a deal was immediately replaced with shame for what that deal cost me, both in money and in self-respect. (Also, it turns out that a lot of places mean it when they say "final sale.")

It wasn't just a bad habit that frustrated me. It changed the way I saw myself.

Helpers in Disguise

Here's what I wish I could have told myself then: bad habits don't make you bad; they make you human.

Life is a lot for everybody, and we all need ways to cope. Sometimes, these coping methods become habits that are ultimately bad for us.

A redefinition of bad habits is in order!

Bad habits are regular and often subconscious behaviors that conflict with our values and interfere with our priorities.

That definition likely makes sense to you, but there's something additional that you need to know: bad habits are "helpers in disguise."

I'm not saying they *actually* help. I'm saying they're *trying* to help. But, like a toddler who makes a mess of the sink and countertop while trying to wash their own hands, bad habits' attempts to help ripple out to unhelpful results.

So, if they're ineffective at best, and damaging at worst, why do they stick around?

Bad habits stick because they're either serving a purpose or meeting a deeper need, even if we're not fully conscientious of how.

Identifying the ways that even your bad habits are helpers is an important step to working on them. Before I teach you how, I need to give you a little kick in the pants.

Revision over Elimination

You will never be bad habit free.

I say this not to depress you, but to help you reframe how you choose to work on your bad habits. Instead of the goal being elimination, it's more about **revision**.

I want to invite you to do so by working on the most common kind of bad habits: those that act as numbing behaviors that so easily suck us in, aka numbing out.

The behaviors that suck us in so easily—so unintentionally—are the ones that often feel the worst. Some examples:

- I didn't *intend* to hide in my pantry eating chocolate chips while avoiding cleaning the kitchen.
- I didn't *mean* to watch 10 YouTube videos in a row instead of drafting that important email to my boss.
- I didn't really *choose* to be on my phone doomscrolling when my kid needed to practice reading with me.

Numbing behaviors are typically the most common bad habits I work on with every single client, whether we planned to or not. The good news is we *all* have these types of habits. Remember, you're a human in an innately stressful world, so we *all* have moments when we cope, and often in ways that aren't productive or even intentional! I'm sure people you wouldn't expect like Oprah, Mel Robbins, or the Dalai Lama have their own go-to bad habits that are *trying* to help by numbing. Again: bad habits do not make *you* bad.

And yet, I don't want you to mistake accepting bad habits as giving up. These habits are bad for many reasons, and it's important to work on them.

The key to revising our bad habits is *not* to quit them cold-turkey. When I did that with my online shopping, guess who suddenly got really into scrolling the news online? This gal. I'm sure you've experienced something similar.

Perhaps in your pursuit to stop playing games on your phone, you've become surprisingly interested in connecting with old friends on Facebook. Perhaps in your desire to quit binge-watching hours of Netflix each night, you've instead found yourself "busy" with emails on your computer. Perhaps in your haste to take Instagram off of your phone, you've become an avid consumer of YouTube shorts.

While there is a case for making certain habits harder to engage in (and I will make one), *truly* revising these habits has to begin *deep*, and then go *practical*. (Yes, even bad habits go deeper!)

Neutralize Bad Habits

The first step in going deep? You have to remove the morality you've attached to your bad habits.

Most people's bad habits are not murder, infidelity, lying, or cheating. So, it's safe to say that the bad habits you'd like to change are not innately immoral. But, we tend to moralize these behaviors because we dislike their effects.

When we moralize, shame gets in the driver's seat. And what did we learn about shame? It doesn't sustainably change behaviors.

This is why before we even begin to work on our bad habits, we have to neutralize them. Doing so will create space for both the curiosity and the compassion you need *first* to understand your negative behaviors, and *then* to shape them.

One of the ways we can achieve this is by humanizing these behaviors. I just did this with the "Oprah, and so on" references a few sections ago, and you can do similarly. *Everyone* has bad habits, even those you greatly admire. You're allowed to be human!

EDIT to Revise

To help with the whole deep then practical process of revising bad habits, follow the EDIT steps.

Steps of Revision: EDIT

E: Examine the habit (understand the habit and identify its pattern(s) [*WHEN* + *THEN* + *AFTER*: WTA]).
D: Disrupt the ease of the habit (delete/diminish the *WHEN*).
I: Insert a better behavior (switch the *THEN*).
T: Train the new action (double down on the *AFTER*).

Please consider one habit you'd especially like to change as we move through these steps. The rest of this chapter will be devoted to the first EDIT step, examine.

Examination happens in phases, each phrased as a question.

> **How to examine your habit:**
>
> 1. **How is your habit "helping?"**
> 2. **How is your habit "hurting?"**
> 3. **What patterns does your habit follow?**

Examination Phase One: How Is Your Habit Helping?

Habits stick when they're effective. Bad habits *are* effective habits, even if we don't love their consequences. To change them we need to understand the purposes they're serving and the deeper needs they're meeting.

Allow me to illustrate understanding with my bad habit of online shopping.

Looking back, I now can see that this wasn't a habit I engaged in because I *wanted* to frivolously spend our money. Sure, the thrill of a deal was alluring, and snapping something up provided a momentary dopamine hit. But, the real reason why that habit stuck around was because it was serving multiple needs.

I wasn't fully aware of it then, but my penchant for online shopping created the break my brain and body desperately needed from the responsibility, sensory input, pressure, and chaos of my all-day-every-day life. It also tapped into a creative part of me that loves to use clothes as a form of personal expression, helped me lean into my interests like interior design, and, honestly, made life feel a little fun when it was hard to come by.

For yourself, think about that bad habit that you'd like to work on. Get curious: ***In what ways is this habit trying to help?***

If you don't understand the *why* behind a bad habit and instead just quit it cold turkey, then two things typically happen: (1) another form of numbing out will take over or (2) the original behavior will resurface either in spurts or in tidal waves.

Both happened to me when I gritted my way through no more online shopping. After quitting, I *still* found myself online, but instead of checking deals it was anything, from the news to my email to Instagram. Inevitably I would cave and go on a sudden shopping bender, which felt both extra shameful and like I was starting back at square one.

Without understanding, patterns will repeat—just under different disguises.

While it feels weirdly validating to understand how bad habits help, these still aren't the kinds of habits we want to stick around. To truly address them, we *must* also acknowledge how bad habits ultimately hurt more than they help.

Examination Phase Two: How Is Your Habit Hurting?

With all this talk of neutralizing and understanding, you may wonder why we should even try to shift these habits. Maybe they're not so bad after all?

They are. It comes down to two big things.

> **Bad habits are bad when they conflict with your values and/or work against your priorities.**

Values

Values are principles that matter deeply to you. They are the core of *who* you are, not just what you *do*. When what you do conflicts with your values, then you have a conflict of identity. That feels bad.

This is why online shopping was a negative habit for me. Online shopping is not innately immoral. I can shop responsibly and in alignment with my values, and often do. However, this behavior became a bad habit when it felt in conflict with *who* I am, particularly as someone who values frugality and wise decision-making. When online shopping became a coping mechanism that hurt more than helped, it officially became a problem.

In all fairness to myself, I didn't take out secret credit cards, I didn't actively hide my purchases from my husband (we shared the same bank account), and I didn't get us in any debt (I made lots of returns). I just spent more and more rashly than was wise, and in ways that felt antithetical to *who* I am.

(PS. If any of those other things were true—and they could have been with time—I'd label that habit more as an addiction, one that may require professional help. Again, the lines between a bad habit and an addiction are fuzzy, and only you can draw them.)

Consider that bad habit you'd like to work on. ***How does it conflict with your personal values and the way you'd like to see yourself?***

Priorities

Priorities are often value-based, but in this context I'd like you to think of priorities as the ways you intend to use your time. Think: responsibilities and to-dos.

While online shopping rarely got in the way of my mom duties, I'd still find myself wasting away the time I originally intended for other things, like reading a book, mopping the floor, replying to emails, or calling a friend. A quick sales scroll would lead to time and opportunity lost. I was left scrambling to make up my delayed tasks and holding an empty self-care bucket.

Hand in hand with deeper negative implications, bad habits cause superficial havoc and to varying extremes. Daily frustrations to bigger life disruptions act as the consequences of our bad habits in ways we can *literally* see, from not following through with what we intended, to not showing up for our people.

I'd argue that what really makes a bad habit "bad" is its **lack of intention.** How many times have you let long moments inch by while scrolling on your phone, when you had no plans to do so? The same thing can be true with playing games, reading, and even organizing. (Remember, bad habits aren't innately immoral, so even the habits that appear good on the outside can be used unintentionally, go against values, and carry negative consequences. Even bad habits are subjective.)

Think about your bad habit again. ***In what ways does this habit occur unintentionally? How does it work against your priorities? What are the consequences you regularly face, thanks to this habit?***

Examination Phase Three: What Patterns Does Your Habit Follow?

Just like supportive habits, bad habits follow a pattern. Thankfully, it's something we are already well familiar with, thanks to the **Sticky Habit Formula:** ***WHEN+THEN+AFTER.***

With the supportive habits you worked on, your WTA became a plan that you intentionally sought out. You may not have been intentionally choosing bad habits, but the WTA formula is still at work. We can use the WTA to interrupt, mold, and even transform bad habits completely. Here's how.

When-Then Pairings for Bad Habits

The When-Then Pairing is alive and well with bad habits. Your bad habit (like a numbing behavior) is the *THEN*, the easiest step to identify. The *WHEN* can be harder to track.

If you struggle to identify what happens *before* your bad habit, you're not alone! These behaviors often carry an almost anesthetic effect, like, "How did I get here?" When bad habits feel so second-nature, sorting them out can be tricky.

But, rest assured that there *are* patterns at play. If bad habits are serving a purpose, they're likely trying to subconsciously help something your brain perceives as wrong, off, uncomfortable, or even threatening—in other words, triggers. These triggers are your *WHEN*s.

While there are some bad habits that have triggers that start externally (e.g., circumstances), and others that are solely internal (e.g., emotions), I find that the majority of triggers are a mix of both. It's not just that running late led you to chew your nails; it's that running late made you feel anxious, and *that* anxiety led to the chewing.

Think of the habit you're revising and start paying attention to what happens before. It's okay if there's more than one thing, but your answer(s) become your *WHEN*(s).

Examples of external *WHEN* triggers:

WHEN my kids fight, *THEN* I . . .
WHEN I get overstimulated by noise, *THEN* I . . .
WHEN my husband doesn't notice things that need to be done, *THEN* I . . .
WHEN I am late, *THEN* I . . .

Examples of internal *WHEN* triggers:

WHEN I feel bored, *THEN* I . . .
WHEN I become stressed and overwhelmed, *THEN* I . . .

WHEN I am avoidant of my to-dos, *THEN* I . . .
WHEN I feel anxious, *THEN* I . . .

Examples of combined external and internal *WHEN* triggers:

WHEN my kids fight, *and* I feel helpless, *THEN* I. . .
WHEN I get overstimulated by noise, *and* I am overwhelmed, *THEN* I . . .
WHEN my husband doesn't notice home tasks, *and* I get angry, THEN I . . .
WHEN I am late, *and* I feel anxious, THEN I . . .

Once you have your answers, keep your bad habit's When-Then Pairing(s) in mind as we uncover the final part of the WTA pattern: *AFTER*.

AFTER

Remember how bad habits are actually helpers in disguise? That they're serving a purpose, however poorly? That's part of the *AFTER*.

Just like some intentional positive reinforcement helps make a good habit stick, the same can happen with a bad habit. Think: dopamine rushes, breaks from reality, time to process, numbing out (however momentarily), and so on. While fleeting, these "helpers" absolutely serve as little feel-good rewards to your brain, just like M&Ms do for toddlers getting potty trained. (Something I'm literally in the middle of doing as I write this book.)

Answer this: ***How is your habit helping?***

Perhaps like me and shopping, your habit gives you a short respite? A rush of feel-good feelings? A break for your brain? A sense of control? Ask yourself, "What purpose is this habit serving?"

Your answers here reveal how your negative behavior is getting reinforced. Remember, habits stick when they're effective. Your *AFTER* fulfills that requirement.

Now that you understand your habit—from its purpose, its harm, and its pattern(s) (WTA!)—now you're ready to disrupt it. (Remember our EDIT steps: examine, disrupt, insert, train.) But first, if you're struggling with the examination step, I have a suggestion.

Train Your Brain: The Three Ns

Bad habits are tricky for many reasons. They're mysteriously automatic, and the shame they bring up may also keep us from trying to solve those mysteries. If you're in that place and you are having a difficult time examining your bad habit, I recommend training your brain to collect needed information via the Three Ns. These steps are optional (and separate from our EDIT steps), but helpful if and when you're stuck.

The Three Ns:

Notice the bad habit in real time and what triggered it.
Name the emotions you're avoiding and what you need.
Next ("What's next?") decide what will really help.

Before I break these steps down, please know that just like we trained our brains to create good habits, we can train our brains to change bad habits. With the Three Ns, that training is most effective when done incrementally. This happens slowly, often over weeks at a time.

BRAIN HACK

To train your brain to revise negative behaviors, be sure to work through the Three Ns one step at a time. Don't move on until you feel comfortable with (and less threatened by) the step you're on.

Notice

Noticing is simply flagging your bad habits *in real time*. I find it helps to call it for what it is: "I am numbing out" or "This is a bad habit." You do this any time you notice the behaviors happening, even if you've already gotten swept away by their numbing powers.

When you are first working to revise a bad habit, noticing is not only the first step—it's the *only* step. Why? In order to fix a habit, we have to trick your brain into working on it in a non-threatening manner.

If your brain thinks that noticing a bad habit means it will have to then *work* to stop the behavior, it will do everything it can to pretend the bad habit isn't happening. But, if we just *notice* the bad habit and stop there, we train our brains to be open and curious (and *not* afraid of doing more work!).

Once you get better at noticing your bad habit, then you can also track when, how, and why it started. Those are the external and internal triggers (*WHEN*s) that we talked about.

Name

Once you've tricked yourself into noticing the behavior and its patterns more often, you are then ready to NAME two things, and in this order:

- **"What emotion(s) am I feeling?"**
- **"What do I really need?"**

External triggers (like our spilled milk example) directly lead to emotions (e.g., rage, overwhelm, or exhaustion). Emotional triggers are often simmering under the surface and just need a little push (like an external trigger) to boil over. To truly understand your bad habit (in this case, yelling over the spilled milk), it's vital that you connect it back to feelings.

Try asking yourself, **"What emotion is this bad habit trying to numb/mask/avoid?"**

If at first it's hard to name your emotional triggers, that's okay! Many clients have to really lean into this phase because naming emotions is not easy. Once you train your brain to get curious, to *notice* the bad habit then *name* the emotion it masks, you'll find the answers gradually start trickling in. There will be patterns and, with time, you'll be able to spot them.[1]

After identifying the emotional triggers, you ***name*** **what you** ***need.***

If you're really out of tune with your needs, it's likely because it's been so. very. long. since you've honored them. Your mind and body are going to stop knocking on a door that never gets answered. Or, they'll just pound the door down with chronic illness, mental health breakdowns, or mommy tantrums.

This is why naming what you need comes *after* you get good at naming your emotions. Not only do the emotions inform what you need but also getting in touch with your mind and body show them that you're listening and will respond.

What you need may surprise you. It may be as momentary as "I need a snack" or "I need a nap." It may be more big picture like "I need more time to myself" or "I need a therapist." Or it may be totally unexpected, "I need to go to a movie" or "I need bangs." (Who am I to judge?)

---

[1] For further support on this, I recommend the wheel of emotions, a visual full of feelings you can use to identify your own. You can find one here: https://www.isu.edu/media/libraries/counseling-and-testing/documents/Wheel-of-Emotions-Handout-(3).pdf.

While writing this book, a major work project left me completely drained. It was one that demanded nearly every moment of my work (and free) time for six months straight. Throughout that time, my brain and body were knocking, *begging* for help, but I simply couldn't fully meet their needs. Once the project ended, I was so thoroughly exhausted I could barely function. (Also: cue more numbing behaviors!) I had to take stock of what I needed. Immediately, I was able to acknowledge that rest must be a top priority, but another answer really surprised me: "I need a hobby."

Be open to what you need! And, if you can't meet those needs right away, that's okay, too. Even the act of acknowledging your needs will show your mind and body you're going to answer the door. Then, you can get creative about other ways to meet the needs you've named.

Naming is really a continuation of the purpose behind noticing—getting in tune with yourself and collecting information. I know it's not an overnight fix, but 99.9% of life isn't. So, stay strong and move slowly.

Next

This phase is about asking yourself, "*What's next?*" Or, to borrow from the WIN-WIN formula in Chapter 11: ***"What's important now?"*** Once you know what's next (including what's important now), you can address the emotions and needs you've named.

Except, that's not where I want you to start. Your brain, which loves the status quo, is going to *hate* doing anything different. No matter how much a bad habit hurts you, your sweet brain is going to want to stick with what feels safe and comfy. So, we've got to once again trick it into being open and malleable.

There's one key to both tricking your brain and choosing what's next. It's something I always teach my clients, and hearing it the first time usually takes them aback: *continue the bad habit*.

Yes, in choosing what's next we will eventually shift to a behavior that better supports your needs. But, initially, *choosing* the same bad habit makes it more intentional. Sometimes you just need a good phone scroll or an emotional support cookie, am I right?!? In truth, we can control most bad habits simply by making the goal "more intention," not elimination.

With a little time and increased confidence ("Look at me! I only scrolled for 20 minutes instead of two hours, because I chose it!"), you'll finally be ready to gently push your brain into the discomfort zone and choose a different "What's *next*," meaning something that isn't a bad habit for you.

If the needs you named are too big to tackle immediately (such as the need for better home systems, to be more seen by your family, to have a hobby, etc.), then your objective is to still give yourself a choice that supports you in the moment. Likely, that will be something that helps you cope better with the emotion you named, from frustration, to sadness, to boredom.

This was true for Hilary, a client I shared about at the end Chapter 9. Hilary wanted to stop scrolling her phone, a behavior we discovered to be far more about numbing out her childhood trauma. We decided to delay working on scrolling until she felt more supported, and that support came through some choices Hilary made: she found a trauma-informed therapist; Hilary spoke to her husband about what was resurfacing for her; then together, they prioritized Hilary taking a daily nature walk sans children to soothe her brain and body. She had a longer path to revising her bad habit, but she was doing so wisely by meeting the most important needs first.

It will take time and work, but with the Three Ns, notice, name, and next, you'll gradually be able to meet your momentary needs and have the clarity to address the more complicated ones.

Never Fully Free

Remember, we will never be bad habit free. That person doesn't exist. Instead, to successfully shape our behaviors we take on a lifelong pursuit of *revising* our bad habits rather than trying to shamefully *eliminate* them.

That revision begins first by examining your habit with some good old-fashioned curiosity. With those answers in hand, you're ready for the next EDIT steps and, coincidentally, the next chapter.

JILL

It took a lot of courage for Jill to open up to me about her eating issues at work. Not only was this habit something that didn't match her health values or disciplined personality, Jill also felt the shame that all women carry who have ever been forced to record a food diary. But, Jill wanted to amend this behavior that was clouding too much of her brain at work so she could instead get clarity on what to do about her job—the original goal of coaching. After teaching Jill the Three Ns, she began with simply noticing the behavior. "Monica," *she told me,* "I'm so astonished! There are a few patterns surrounding when I'm unintentionally eating that I didn't notice until now." *Those patterns included the* WHEN *being the start of her prep period—one that happened directly after the most intense class of the day—and other* WHENs *happened more sporadically, but usually involved a tough moment with a student.*

Jill moved on to naming the internal triggers: stress and exhaustion. Then, Jill asked herself what she needed next: more support, more rest, and more stability. The school was short-staffed so we couldn't fix the lack of support; but, we could find ways for Jill to work on better supporting herself. We decided to do so by adding in habits that Jill could do at home that would provide more rest and stability, while also implementing other habits she could use at work to replace the mindless munching. Both required the next level of revising her bad habit—and Jill was ready.

TAKEAWAYS: Bad habits are "helpers in disguise." To revise (not eliminate) bad habits, we need to follow the EDIT steps, beginning with answering the examination questions: How is your bad habit helping, how is it hurting, and what pattern(s) (WTA) does it follow? If answers are hard to come by, train your brain to collect information by following the Three Ns: notice, name, and next.

TAKE THOUGHT: Consider the bad habit you want to work on and answer these questions: In what ways is this habit trying to help? How does it actually hurt? What typically triggers this behavior?

TAKE ACTION: Notice the bad habit in real time and collect information.

NOTE: For more (printables, recommended books, complementary podcast episodes, etc.), remember to check out the free and included Sticky Habit resources, available online at https://stickyhabitsbook.com/resources:

Chapter 13

Using Existing Patterns to Train Bad Habits

Learn: How to follow the EDIT steps to practically revise a bad habit's WHEN + THEN + AFTER (WTA)

I used to be a major thumb sucker as a child, well past when it was socially acceptable for most children. As a second grader, I couldn't *not* suck my thumb while on the bus, in class, or on the playground. My parents worried about me getting made fun of just as much as they were concerned about cosmetic damage, plus the extensive and expensive orthodontics that would surely follow. (Spoiler: they did, headgear and all.)

Even though this habit was unsanitary and not age appropriate, it did serve a purpose: sucking my thumb soothed me through moments of fear, anxiety, and even boredom. It was a habit in its purest form, effectively doing its job in the short term while ignoring the negative ramifications in the long term.

My general WTA looked something like this:

W = *WHEN* I experience a negative emotion . . .
T = *THEN* I suck my thumb . . .
A = *AFTER* I feel better.

But, more specific triggers looked like this:

W = *WHEN* my teacher seems annoyed with me, or a boy makes fun of me, or I feel bored on the bus, or I am sleepy after dinner . . .
T = *THEN* I suck my thumb . . .
A = *AFTER* I feel comforted and less worried, sad, and/or bored.

Understanding this behavior would have helped remove some of the thumb sucker shame I carried (I did know it wasn't a cool thing, okay?), and it also would have provided the information I needed to reform the behavior.

What Comes Next

After examining your bad habit and identifying its pattern(s) (WTA), what do you do? It's time for the next EDIT steps, starting with disrupt! The remaining steps of the revision process each work hand in hand with your bad habit's WTA.

Steps of Revision: EDIT

E: Examine the habit (understand the habit and identify its pattern(s) (WTA)).
D: Disrupt the ease of the habit (delete/diminish the *WHEN*).
I: Insert a better behavior (switch the *THEN*).
T: Train the new action (double down on the *AFTER*).

Small Picture Versus Big Picture Revision

A quick note before we move into the next step in the EDIT process.

Revising bad habits includes seeing them through two different lenses: small picture and big picture.

The small picture lens entails identifying negative WTAs that can be actively worked on. Guess what? That's what you've been learning to do with the EDIT steps. (Yay!) The big picture lens means acknowledging that there are deeper issues at play with most bad habits, and those issues need to be addressed in order to effectively reform negative behaviors as a whole.

For example: maybe you yell when your kids fight. We will improve how to handle that trigger better when they fight (because they will). However, perhaps what you really *need* overall is for more help from your spouse so you have increased bandwidth to handle the demands of parenting. Or you need to process some childhood issues that the fighting dredges up for you. Or you need better household systems, the kind that go hand in hand with the main issues your kids tend to fight about.

These types of concerns will require more time, creativity, and persistence to address. We will look at big picture fixes in the following chapters. Meanwhile, this chapter will focus on strategies you can use with the small picture: considering specific habits' WTAs and how to practically revise them.

Disrupt the Ease of the Habit (Delete/Diminish the *WHEN*)

Because bad habits tend to happen automatically, they almost seem like they're too easy. They often don't require our energy or active decision-making to stick around. So, we make bad habits *harder* with these two options: delete or diminish the *WHENs*. Either or both of these steps disrupt the ease of the bad habit.

Ideally, *deleting* the trigger to your bad habit is the most straightforward option. If you don't have the *WHEN*, you don't have the *THEN*!

Admittedly, this only works with a few types of bad habits, those that have a very strong, simple, and perhaps even nonemotional, external cues, like chewing gum after a meal despite having severe jaw issues, or looking at your phone every time a notification comes up. In these cases, you take the bad habit off the table by removing what comes before, like no longer allowing gum in the house or removing notifications from your phone. You can see the effectiveness of removing the *THEN* (the bad habit) by deleting its *WHEN* (the trigger).

Most often, deleting a bad habit's trigger won't be that easy. However, you usually can at least weaken it. That's the *diminish* option.

Let's get back to the example of yelling at your kids. If I asked you if it were possible to remove the *WHEN*—the trigger to your yelling—you might sarcastically respond, "Sure, I'll just make my kids disappear!"

We can't all be like Kevin McCallister and make our families disappear. That said, here are some things we *can* do to delete or diminish the *WHEN* triggers with kids and yelling:

- Come up with a better morning routine to eliminate the getting-ready-for-school chaos that cues your drill sergeant reactions.
- Improve your screen time system, as yelling is often connected with unclear or lackluster rules about devices.
- Get more sleep or alone time, as the main trigger for your raised voice is feeling straight-up exhausted.

As with yelling, you absolutely *can* eliminate or weaken most bad habit triggers, but doing so will often require more big picture effort as well. Again, we'll return to exploring that type of labor in Chapter 14. In the meantime, use the weakening strategy to diminish the ease of the habit by making it harder, thereby disrupting its flow.

You can do that by roughing up your When-Then Pairing so it doesn't run like a well-oiled machine. Do you remember the "lowering the hurdle" tip in Chapter 9, where, like a track star cheating at the hurdles, you make a good, new habit *easier*? You can use that same analogy and *raise the hurdle*, making a bad habit *harder* to leap over—like a naughty competitor hijacking the race from her opponent.

By mid-second grade, my parents had tried everything to help me stop sucking my thumb. I wanted to quit this habit, too, so I willingly signed up for all tactics, including icky-tasting polish on my nails and special incentives for abstaining. The only thing that worked was removing the ease of placing my thumb in my mouth via something called *the cage*.

I have no idea if this is even an option these days, but my parents took me to an orthodontist who cemented three sharp metal prongs onto the back of my front teeth. Every time I went to put my thumb in my mouth, I'd get poked instead. It was uncomfortable, but it was effective. I technically *could* manipulate my mouth to put my thumb in a different spot or use smaller fingers; however, it simply wasn't easy anymore—so I stopped, and even after the cage was removed, I never sucked my thumb again. (I promise!)

Raising the hurdle comes in handy with numbing behaviors that involve electronic devices, from phones to game consoles. You can rough up those habits and make them harder to do by placing locks or time limits on your devices, or even putting them in harder to reach places (e.g., not your back pocket).

My podcast manager, Taylor, couldn't stop picking at her nails and the surrounding skin beds to the point where they would bleed. It was an anxious habit she had had since she was small, and she was embarrassed by how her nailbeds looked. To make this behavior harder, Taylor started getting her nails done by a friend who learned to do manicures. Taylor now either does them herself or gets her nails done at the salon. Raising the hurdle by making it harder to pick at her nails has made the bad habit disappear—that and inserting another good habit (exercise) to support her anxious tendencies. (More on that next . . .)

Even a little more grit on your cue disrupts the flow between being triggered and automatically reacting. However you do it—delete or diminish—think about how you can disrupt your bad habits' flow by modifying your When-Then Pairings.

Insert a Better Behavior (Switch the *THEN*)

Like Glinda from *Wicked*, we may desire to carry a magic wand that fixes bad habits with a simple wave, but we simply don't have that kind of power. We have to take care of our problems ourselves, which will require some creativity, effort, and persistence. This is where the Insert step comes in. You've got the same *WHEN* (trigger), but can you replace the *THEN* (response)?

Let's go back to yelling at your kids. Your children aren't going anywhere, and your triggers will take some time to diminish (like the kids learning how to put their stuff away), so it's likely that some triggers will remain.

Here's where some creativity is needed. What is a different type of *THEN* you can switch out with this yelling habit? We want a habit that is supportive, gives you space to regulate, and grants your brain time to think.

I wouldn't advise that "Just don't yell" be the new *THEN*. Relying solely on grit isn't going to cut it. Nor would I recommend initially inserting behaviors that require a lot of energy like "Go on a walk" or "Write in my journal," even if they could technically help create the same release that yelling does. With this kind of habit—as with most bad habits—what you really have is a response problem. In other words, you *react* instead of *respond*.

I call the space between the trigger and response (i.e., the space between your When-Then Pairing) the *Response Gap*. This short timeframe is your chance to process what's happening and choose how to respond. Unfortunately with a bad habit like yelling at your kids, the Response Gap is almost nothing.

I highly recommend inserting a new *THEN* that extends the Response Gap. Even if at first it's just an extra second, with practice you can widen that gap. Eventually you will have enough time to think, make a choice, and insert a good habit that actually helps.

In his book, *Man's Search for Meaning*, Viktor Frankl, an Austrian neurologist, psychiatrist, and Holocaust survivor, wrote, "Between stimulus and response there is a space. In that space is our power to choose our response. In our response lies our growth and our freedom."[1]

We often feel powerless with our bad habits because they don't feel *chosen*. They're our basest selves reacting to the stressors of life in ways that ultimately don't help, nor feel good. To get our higher selves—our thinking brains—back on board, we can create mini-habits that stretch out the Response Gap, ones that help us earn back our power to choose, something that will feel akin to freedom.

Train your brain to extend the Response Gap, the space between a trigger and your reactionary bad habit. BRAIN HACK

I will have much more to say about the essential, truly life-giving power of emotional regulation in Chapter 14, but consider a few of these mini-habits to insert as a new in-the-moment *THEN* to replace any of the bad habits you are working on, from yelling to scrolling:

- **The Deep Breath:** Nervous system regulation 101 all starts with breathing, the body's only function that is both voluntary (like moving a hand) and involuntary (like a beating heart). Breathing happens on its own, but we can also control it. In doing so, our bodies kick into the parasympathetic drive of our nervous system, one that pauses the runaway train feelings. We all are familiar with the calming power of breathing, but when

[1]Viktor Frankl, *Man's Search for Meaning* (Beacon Press, 2006).

we are in a reactive moment or running on autopilot, doing a breathing exercise may feel like too much. So instead, I advise my clients to start with the Deep Breath. It's simply that: one long deep breath. It can take 3 seconds, it can take 10. It's less about the specificity of how it's executed and more about lengthening your Response Gap. When you notice your *WHEN* happening, take the Deep Breath. With time, you can make the breath longer, you can add in more breaths, you can even do a breathing exercise or tack on some somatic movements (see next). But honestly? Most of the time one Deep Breath is all many women need to slow down the auto-cogs in their brains, step in, and make a choice about how they want to handle the trigger in a different way. It takes some training and time, but it's wildly effective.

- **Somatic movements:** Somatic means "related to the body," and this is also nervous system 101! We can use our bodies to calm down our brains enough that we can *respond* instead of react. Go back to your childhood self who, when upset, loved to be held tightly, to be rocked, to be hummed to. Those are somatic movements, the kind that calm your fight-or-flight, autopilot brain. Options can include placing your hands over your heart (a favorite of many of my clients), tapping your hands against part of your body (on the chest, on the legs, on the face, etc.), wrapping your arms around yourself and squeezing tight, rocking your shoulders side to side, or swaying your whole body back and forth. There are countless others just a quick Google search away, but I always recommend going with whatever feels the most simple and natural. It doesn't have to be novel each time—sticking with what works is actually the best course.
- **Walk away:** This seems simple—and it is—but if you're in reactive mode, walking away may be too much effort. However, I find removing myself from the space I'm getting

triggered works well when coupled with the Deep Breath or other somatic movements. Like any of these new *THEN*s, the more you do it, the easier it gets, and soon you don't even really have to think through it—you just find yourself walking away.

These are the three options I recommend starting with in real time. There may be others that appeal to you, and I welcome you to brainstorm about them in the Crackdown Plan we have for you as a printable in the free online resources. I will have more to say on the bigger picture solutions—ones that connect back to this whole nervous system thing, too—again, starting in Chapter 14. Sorry to be a tease.

But, this is where we begin: simple, regulating habits that act as the foundation for deeper, longer-term work. Like any new skill set, be persistent. Many of these options will feel unnatural at first, but they won't with time. You are in training mode! Which brings us to the final step to EDIT a bad habit.

Train a New Action (Double Down on the *AFTER*)

Revising bad habits is hard. So is getting our brains on board with change, and widening the Response Gap. It's all challenging! In the favored words of my four sisters, your brain is going to go "cray-cray," meaning it's not going to like even the simplest of changes you make to your long-standing WTAs. Your brain *will resist* your attempts to rough up your *WHEN* (trigger) or switch out your *THEN* (response) with the Deep Breath. This is why you have to train your brain to *like* these changes. How? By doubling down on what comes *AFTER*. This goes back to our brain hacking ways of creating all the feel-good chemicals that prime the brain to desire something, even if it feels disruptive and uncomfortable at first.

> **Use positive reinforcement to train your brain to be more receptive and drawn to responding differently to meet your deeper needs (i.e., inserting a different habit or taking a deep breath instead of the bad habit).** BRAIN HACK

Luckily, this is quite simple: talk to yourself like a small child and praise every inch of effort you make and success you achieve with all the gusto you can muster, exclamation points abounding:

- *"Look at you! You started yelling, but stopped yourself and took a Deep Breath!"*
- *"Go, Taylor, go! I see you fighting against that desire to pick your nails by walking around the room instead—you're doing it!"*
- *"High five! [Yes, you can high five yourself.] That was a tough moment of resisting scrolling your phone. I see how you're now reading a book instead—'That's like me!'"*

There's power in speaking kind words to yourself, aloud or not. However you do it, you've got to double down on both noticing and encouraging *any* sign of progress. This may feel strange at first, or even phony, but your brain *loves* positive reinforcement. I recommend having some go-to mantras to encourage yourself, such as the now classic, "That's like me!"

And, just like with training good habits, you can literally reward yourself for efforts extended and changes completed as a form of *AFTER*. Yes, I do mean even when you *try*—even if later than desired or with lackluster initial results, still reward yourself. Same goes for when you are successful to any degree, and I mean *any*.

While we still want to stay away from rewards that take a lot of energy, think of some nice but easy ones you can install in the moment: filling in a habit tracker, giving yourself a literal pat on the back, watching your favorite *Saturday Night Live* clip, sucking on a piece of dark chocolate, calling your mom or bestie, or blasting a celebratory song.

As with positive reinforcement when installing a good habit, this isn't something you're going to have to do the rest of your life while revising bad habits. When it's effective, the *AFTER* will naturally fall away. But, it's also a great tool to return to whenever a bad habit sneaks back into your life. Because those dummies like doing that.

While fortunately I'm not a closeted 40-year old thumb sucker, online shopping is still something I occasionally have to work on. The whole EDIT series of steps aren't necessarily needed now when I notice I've once again checked out of an entire "on sale" cart; but, I can extract certain steps and tools to help me understand *why* this happened (usually I'm stressed out), gently work myself through some alternative coping mechanisms, and celebrate hard the next time I manage to stop myself mid-sale scroll. When those victories happen, I literally stop, take a Deep Breath, and say to myself, "Good job!" I sometimes even follow up with watching a video from my favorite YouTube channel.

You didn't know it in real time, but these bad habits were trained into your brain; you can train them out of it, too. Double down on what comes *AFTER*, and you are well on your way!

Helpful Resources

As mentioned, you can get a Crackdown Plan as a free printable available with our online resources. This printable helps you follow the EDIT system to come up with your own plan to revise your bad habit under the small picture lens. I recommend taping your plan somewhere near the environment where the bad habit typically occurs, all so it's top of mind.

Also in these resources, you can download a series of habit trackers that are different than most on the market. They're called *Sticky Habits Trackers*, and they can be applied to train both good and bad habits. Instead of traditional trackers that are chains where if you miss a single day you hate yourself and quit, these trackers are pictures where you can gradually fill in little segments each time you celebrate a victory in either establishing a new habit or reforming an old one. With time, you'll see the colors build to a beautiful finished product, and I'm not just talking about the picture. Just like your Crackdown Plan, tape up a Sticky Habits Tracker where it's easiest to color in.

Both of these resources are available to you at https://stickyhabitsbook.com/resources.

While we've learned a great deal about what you can do to revise habits in the here and now, we're going to cover the deeper and broader work needed for true revision, in the next and final two chapters of Part Five—yes, the ones I said I'd eventually get to!

But first, let's check in on Jill.

JILL

Jill had tracked the patterns and the efficacies of her emotional eating at work. With that knowledge (and compassion!) behind her, she moved through the EDIT *steps, starting with the most common* WHEN*: at the start of her prep period, right after her hardest class. We began with inserting the Deep Breath at this time of day. Jill acknowledged that this simple act was surprisingly difficult for her brain at first. However, thanks to easing in and praising herself every time she tried, Jill knew taking the breath didn't mean she couldn't eat—she just did so with more presence and intention. With time, the space between her* WHEN *and* THEN *(i.e., the Response Gap) began to grow. Jill found it easier and more instinctual to take the breath; in fact, she could even take a few. And then, almost without intending to, Jill began to reach for other things that helped her cope better instead: from reading for a bit, to walking outside to a bench on campus and taking a moment for herself. Thanks to removing morality from the habit, Jill was surprised to find that sometimes she could indeed use food to cope, but in a way that felt truly soothing and helpful, instead of shameful and numbing. With each moment of choice and celebration ("That's like me!"), Jill found the shackles* *of unintentional eating loosening, and on some days, even falling away. To have them fall off for good, we had to work on other bigger picture things: emotional regulation and systems at home.*

TAKEAWAYS: Now that you've examined (E) your bad habit and identified its WTA, you are ready to follow through with the remaining EDIT steps to revise your habit in real time: D: Disrupt the ease of the habit (delete/diminish the *WHEN*); I: Insert a better behavior (switch the *THEN*); T: Train the new action (double down on the *AFTER*). These steps harness existing patterns to revise bad habits' WTAs. This is the small picture work. Big picture comes next.

TAKE THOUGHT: How could you make your habit harder to reach for? Which of the in-the-moment strategies appeal to you to replace your *THEN*? What is a way you can see yourself more naturally reinforcing your attempts to revise?

TAKE ACTION: Practice extending your Response Gap by taking the Deep Breath.

NOTE: For more (printables, recommended books, complementary podcast episodes, etc.), remember to check out the free and included Sticky Habit resources, available online at https://stickyhabitsbook.com/resources:

Chapter 14

Big Picture Solutions: Nervous System

Learn: How supporting emotional regulation is essential to revising habits

While my online shopping looked like I was hopelessly devoted to the pursuit of a good deal, in reality my bad habit was much more about how dysregulated I was and how I needed more help at home. Working with my bad habit's *WHEN + THEN + AFTER* pattern (WTA) helped to a degree, but for a more lasting fix, I had to look at the big picture. Until I identified and dug out the roots of my bad habits, those behaviors weren't going anywhere long term.

Bad Habits Require Bigger Shifts

Larger efforts are often necessary to properly revise bad habits, from picking at your split ends to playing games on your phone. Some of this will require additional support from friends, family, and even coaches and therapists, but you can still do much of it on your own.

If you've tried to reform the same bad habit over and over, don't despair! The ship may feel like it's sinking, but you don't have to go down with it. There are lifeboats ready and willing to carry you through, and a better ship is coming. You simply have to take that leap into one of the lifeboats.

I find that however helpful the EDIT steps are for retraining a bad habit, it'll all only act as a momentary plug to a major hole unless you consider *why* the proverbial gash appeared in the first place. What is making your ship sink? *That's* what ultimately needs to be fixed, and this insight may require deeper, broader work.

The hole in your habit ship is often a combination of two major categories:

- Emotional regulation support (aka nervous system)
- Invisible labor support (aka home systems)

This chapter will be devoted to the nervous system, and Chapter 15 will focus on home systems.

Emotional Regulation

When I started my podcast in 2016, publicly talking about mental health was a new (and vulnerable!) thing. Laying bare my own struggles with eating disorders, depression, and anxiety welcomed people into my little fold online, even if my personal revelations unpleasantly surprised some of my loved ones. (Sorry!)

As a community, we hit the ground running. We had hard conversations about still-taboo topics. As I interviewed what eventually became hundreds of people—from everyday women sharing their new hobby to bestselling authors teaching their life-changing principles—every single person's journey toward progress inevitably meant working through difficult things that affected their mental health. Over and over again, it was evident that so much of life (and our own thriving or floundering through it) is connected to *how* we move through the challenging emotions we face.

Eventually, I learned of a field of study that encompasses how we process what we experience: emotional regulation. I'll save you the original 3,000 words I wrote on why and how, but suffice to say I received an intense tutelage in all things regulation thanks to my children's varied neurodivergent struggles. Their intense issues—unique to each one of them—all connect back to emotional regulation, and alongside that, the necessity of using the nervous system to better support their pursuit to be healthy, happy humans.

There are people far smarter and more experienced than I who can teach you about regulation. I'm talking about full books on the topic, and many of them! Please reference my online resources for a fuller list, but I would especially recommend: *Joy is My Justice* by Dr. Tanmeet Sethi, *What Happened to You* by Dr. Bruce Perry and Oprah Winfrey, *The 5 Resets* by Dr. Aditi Nerurkar, *Burnout* by Emily and Amelia Nagoski, and *Tiny Humans, Big Emotions* by Alyssa Blask Campbell and Lauren Elizabeth Stauble.

My education gradually led to these books (among others), but it started with a mental health professional who was working with us to help a child stuck in dysregulation. Since this was 2020 and nobody in my day-to-day life was talking about the nervous system yet, I felt like I was learning a whole new language. While this information alone could easily fill chapters, I'll share *my* simplified explanation of the nervous system and then what it has to do with bad habits.

Before I do, please keep in mind that while what I share is well-informed and in good faith (and looked over by a certified, practicing therapist), I'm not a doctor, therapist, or mental health professional. I encourage you to recruit experts from any of those fields if the basics I share here set off light bulbs for you, and you need more support to navigate it.

What is the Nervous System?

Our brains and bodies are interconnected with something called a *nervous system*. Our bodies function like the inside of a computer housing different parts serving different functions, with wires interconnecting it all. We are essentially living, breathing, walking computers with our own communication and operation systems.

The brain acts as our main control center, with the spinal cord serving as the communicator to the rest of our body via nerve networks. However, communication goes both directions—from the brain to the body and from the body to the brain. When our bodies feel safe, our thinking comes from the highest part of our brain—the prefrontal cortex. This is an area just behind our forehead where we can access clear thinking and self-control. That's healthy regulation! Dysregulation is when our thoughts and behaviors come from the brainstem—the amygdala—an area of our primal brains trained to react in true fight-flight-or-freeze fashion. When someone is dysregulated, they can feel flooded with out-of-control emotions (and also behaviors), but they can also shut down.

It's a normal, human thing to experience dysregulation. The goal isn't for all thoughts to come from the safe, higher part of our brains. Instead, the goal is to be able to calm our nervous systems when needed, to move from the brain stem to the prefrontal cortex, and for that process to feel manageable and, eventually, instinctive. We typically learn how to do this quite naturally (if we live in safe environments with regulated caregivers) as we grow from tantrum-throwing toddlers to level-headed adults.

Dysregulation is a problem when it happens often or we get stuck there for prolonged periods without resolution. Persistent states of dysregulation can happen during stressful "survival seasons," but can also stem from neurodifferences, histories with trauma, or upbringings that weren't emotionally safe. (If any of those sound familiar, it's worth looking into trained professionals to get the proper help you deserve.)

Regulation Meets Habits

Even those of us without persistent histories of dysregulation can track how our bad habits connect back to it. Our brainstems volunteer easy "fixes" to what they perceive as threats—and yes, those threats could be an overwhelming to-do list just as much as a screaming boss. Since we are animals at our core, you don't have to experience a major trauma or disruption to trigger survival reactions.

This also helps explain why bad habits can be so sticky. When they're numbing in nature and/or require low energy, they can effectively soothe the nervous system. At least while in that moment.

How is your penchant for yelling, chewing your nails, or endlessly scrolling *really* about being emotionally dysregulated? How are these bad habits signs of your brain reacting from the brain stem? What does it all have to do with your past, from being raised in a turbulent home to your own experiences with trauma that have rattled the ease by which your body can go from shaken up to still?

It's also wise to consider how your good habits help support a healthy nervous system. This can include preemptive support, like a daily habit that calms the brain and body (walking, meditation, etc.) and active support, like *WHEN* dysregulation hits, *THEN* a bad habit tries to step in to "help," but you insert a regulating habit instead. (Reference some of the strategies I shared at the end of Chapter 15, like the Deep Breath.)

Nervous system regulation comes up with every single client I've ever worked with. Even if we don't specifically use terms like *prefrontal cortex*, working on habits means learning how to access healthy emotional regulation. To do so yourself, you have to first understand your own unique signs of dysregulation.

How Your Body Speaks

My mission is to help women feel like themselves—happy! But women can't get there if they aren't able to maintain a healthy loop between the brain and the body.

I'm not naturally a touchy-feely person; I lean more toward the logical than the sensory. While I'm okay now, my years of disordered eating detached so much of my brain from my body. In the past, the only way I knew something was wrong was when my body was screaming at me—from losing half the hair on my head as an extremely anemic newlywed to experiencing fainting spells when something was off with my heart during my last pregnancy.

I find that I'm not alone in this. Thanks to the ongoing responsibilities they carry, so many women have learned to ignore their own needs until it's their norm. Body issues among women are pervasive, leading to a range of detachment between brain and body. I feel that we can't overstate how much these issues affect self-attunement for women.

In my pursuit to put myself on my *own* list and help women do the same, I have learned the necessity of paying better attention to what signals our bodies are sending. And, as part of that, it is vital to understand how regulation and dysregulation *feel*.

You likely experience symptoms of dysregulation you didn't even recognize as such. For example:

- A clenched jaw
- A pounding headache
- Shallow breathing
- A rapid heartrate
- Raised shoulders
- Uncontrollable tears
- Frenetic productivity
- Numbness
- A fuzzy head

My sister, a therapist who specializes in trauma, has shared that her clients tend to vacillate hyperfunctioning (read: over) and hypofunctioning (read: under). They either outrun their emotions in pursuit of avoiding them, or numb them out through mindless behaviors. However, both sides avoid emotions because when they hit, they feel scary and unsafe.

She also said that trauma isn't always what happened to you, it's what *didn't* happen to you, too. This means that those from more "stable" homes can still find many reasons to hide from their emotions. Perhaps your family pushed for perfection or you were never allowed to have a bad day or express a hard emotion. Regardless of if your childhood was "traumatizing," if you didn't feel safe enough to be dysregulated, then you never learned regulation.

Good News

You *can* learn regulation, and in ways that change the very cells of your brain.[1] It's neuroplasticity at work.

To help begin this learning process, answer these questions so you know what you're working with:

- What does it feel like *in your body* when you can't process your emotions?
- What does it feel like when you are regulated?

Cheat sheet on the last one: when you're regulated, you likely feel more calm, stable, and embodied. From your steady heartbeat to your relaxed shoulders, you feel like "you."

If emotions are *extra* hard for you (note: I'm raising my own hand here), start with a general sense of curiosity. As suggested

[1] Nicole R. Giuliani, Emily M. Drabant, Roshni Bhatnagar, and James J. Gross, "Emotion Regulation and Brain Plasticity: Expressive Suppression Use Predits Anterior Insula Volume," *Neuroimage* 58, no. 1 (2011): 10–15. https://doi.org/10.1016/j.neuroimage.2011.06.028.

with the Three Ns, get into the habit of *noticing*, *naming*, and deciding what's *next* with your nervous system. This may be all new territory for you, including this interplay of brain and body that you may have toned down or shut out for years.

Like everything else we've learned, with time and practice you'll be able to track patterns that you can better disrupt in the moment. And with more time, insert stabilizing habits that help you feel more like yourself before, during, or after a moment (or period) of dysregulation.

Your habits can hurt, it's true. But they can also help. What you've learned and worked on thanks to this book are all part of this bigger picture of better supporting the nervous system.

I know I've done my job with a client when she no longer needs me to point out the voices from her head and her body. She is already listening *and* she's responding. This is a healthy nervous system at work. And that's where you're headed!

JILL

Thanks to Jill having an adult son with autism and being a 30+ year special education teacher, she was well familiar with the interplay of the nervous system and emotional regulation—and years before that knowledge had names and expertise. The thing is, her pursuit to help those under her care to better manage their nervous systems had come at the expense of her own. Jill had to admit that she was simply worn out and worn down from her decades of work. While she still held a passion for her students, her time to continue as a full-time teacher was coming to an end. She wanted to retire on a high note, not a burnt-out one. To help her move through that process, and to better assist her in the meantime, Jill needed to better prioritize habits that would regulate her before, during, and after work.

Jill was already an early bird—getting up at 5 a.m.—so I didn't recommend getting up any earlier to add in more supportive habits.

Instead, we paired up what she already did, like by ensuring she was grounded and present during her breakfast meal, that she rocked side to side while brushing her teeth, and she listened to soothing music on her way into work. Each of these habits were regulating, but easy to work in. At school, Jill continued her regulating habits: the Deep Breath, some down time, and the regular bench break to her teaching rhythm. Now, after work, Jill was ready to add in some decompressing walks at a local reservoir on her way home, starting with a baseline of just 10 minutes on the path. As these additional regulating habits were added, Jill found less and less of a drive to mindlessly munch at work. The habit wasn't totally gone, but it wasn't as omnipresent as it had sometimes been in the past. She felt more hope and less fear overall.

TAKEAWAYS: Bad habits require big picture work, starting with supporting emotional regulation via the nervous system. Our bodies are walking, living computers with their own operating and communicating systems that interconnect the brain and body. When there's a disconnect, dysregulation occurs with heightening emotions and behaviors (like bad habits). To revise bad habits in lasting ways, we need to understand how our individual nervous system functions, what helps us regulate, and how to use habits to help.

TAKE THOUGHT: How are your bad habits connected to dysregulation? Which habit would you like to better prioritize as a form of preemptive regulation?

TAKE ACTION: Notice one way your body speaks to you when dysregulated, and one when regulated.

(continued)

(continued)

NOTE: For more (printables, recommended books, complementary podcast episodes, etc.), remember to check out the free and included Sticky Habit resources, available online at https://stickyhabitsbook.com/resources:

Chapter 15

Big Picture Solutions: Home Systems

Learn: How supporting invisible labor at home frees women up to create habits that stick

With three little kids literally clawing for my attention all day every day, two of them having sensory-triggered meltdowns every few minutes, and a husband that was working so much my oldest called him by his first name instead of Dad, I was more than ready for my Saturday morning run.

Despite thinking I had communicated about it properly to Brad ahead of time, I woke up to him getting dressed in his business casual attire like the diligent work soldier that he was. I chewed my lip and spoke up, "I thought I was going to get to go on a run?" Brad looked pained—clearly torn between choosing his work boss or his home boss. Within a span of three minutes, we had a rapid "discussion" where it was "compromised" that I had 30 minutes to run. (Read: we fought.) I changed into my workout clothes, and the toddlers and the baby were practically thrown at Brad as I ran out the front door, shouting over my shoulder before I slammed it shut, "I never get time to myself!"

I have a *very* good husband. One of the best men on earth, truly. Brad is kind, considerate, aware, and in tune with how I'm doing. When his work hours are done, he rolls up his sleeves to labor alongside me in the home without me having to order him around. I'd consider Brad an equal partner in my life.

And yet, even for us, one of the most long-standing stressors on our marriage has been the disparity concerning the labor performed in our home.

Admittedly, I initially signed up for it. I knew before we even said "I do" that I wanted to be a stay-at-home mother while our kids were young and then later, once the kids were older, to have a job that allowed me to be home by the time the school day ended. (We are currently existing between both of those options.) Living this out has been both a privilege and a challenge, and not just for me. Each member of our family has made sacrifices, both personally and financially.

Note: I say this all while fully acknowledging that both partners working full-time also entails major trade-offs and sacrifices. There is no easy way to raise a family. Also, studies show that even when both partners from cisgendered couples work full-time, women still primarily take on the labor at home—a kind of labor that honestly lasts all day, thanks to the mental components alone. This is often referred to as *the second shift*, with women taking on caretaking tasks once they're home from their paying jobs. You can be working and still fill the role as the primary parent and/or the primary one taking on the invisible labor of your home.

Being the primary caretaker for our children has entailed taking on the lion's share of invisible labor that goes into running a household. It's something I chose. I both valued and accepted that disparity at the start of our marriage (at the ripe old age of 21, mind you). However, what I didn't expect was how truly all-consuming, intensive, and yet invisible this labor is, and how invisible it would make *me* feel. It's this feeling that created years of growing resentment and eventually despair. Also, there was the matter of intense self-neglect, one we all ended up paying for.

Invisible Labor Support

I started this book by detailing why women *must* do habits differently thanks to the invisible labor we carry. Now, I need to end it in a sort of full-circle fashion by speaking to the undeniable need women *still* have to better share in this labor, starting with the home.

You can't wait to prioritize and support yourself until after household systems get better. However, it is essential that things at home—and I have found this to be true for *every* home—eventually shift in order to make it possible for you to be a happy human, long term.

It must be acknowledged that good marriages (and with that, good men[1]) easily fall into these patterns. Perhaps, like us, you didn't intend for the loads to be so different in your marriage, but they just happened. My favorite example of this is how many wives automatically find themselves in charge of buying birthday gifts for their husbands' parents as soon as the marriage certificate is signed. The fact that your marriage and your home may be in this space doesn't mean your relationship is doomed to fail. But, you do have to be willing to be a disrupter (or a Revolutionizer, right?) in order to prevent that.

What I'm asking may feel less like stopping a leak and more like preventing the *Titanic* from sinking. For some women, making changes to their home feels is in the camp of "far too little and far, far too late." I get it! But what if you tried anyway? What if you decided that it's never too late, and even the smallest of changes can have a tremendous impact? Trying won't fix everything

[1] A quick acknowledgment that what I'm sharing here is pretty heteronormative. If this doesn't apply to your partnership, or even if you have one, please know that much of what I share will still apply to the home labor you carry.

overnight (nothing will), and there may be some things and some relationships that are too broken to mend, but it's time to find out. It's time to try.

A Needed Shift

You may recall Rebecca, the teacher who made a habit of walking during her prep period. Rebecca had come a long way! She learned to talk to herself with kindness, and made consistent exercise a priority. But there was an obstacle that kept holding her back, even though it was something she originally chose: Rebecca's family did next to nothing to help with the home.

Even though Rebecca worked full-time, she was still solely responsible for everything household-related: from cleaning the bathrooms, to doing the laundry, to managing kids' homework and extracurriculars, to the never-ending cycle of keeping her people fed. Sure, the children had chores. Sure, her husband would chip in when asked and did oversee most of the yard work. And sure, for many years this is how Rebecca chose to contribute to her family.

At first, these dynamics were necessary. While the children were very young and her husband traveled for work, Rebecca took a pay cut to be at a school that allowed her to be home soon after the final bell. This change enabled Rebecca to take the lead on everything at home. And she was happy to do it!

But now, Rebecca was just so dang tired all. the. time. Also, her kids were getting older. Rebecca wanted to raise successful adults, not just children housed in adult-sized bodies. She knew to do right by them as their mother, her kids had to learn the very real, but often overlooked, skill sets of managing a home and themselves. And just as much, she wanted to have some real time for herself, something she hadn't had for as long as she could remember. She wanted a hobby, dang it! Not just to blow off some steam, but to keep her feelings of resentment in check, feelings that were showing up far more than she cared to admit.

What used to work was no longer working. Rebecca couldn't manage the home all by herself and needed everyone else to step up. It all had to start with a sit-down conversation: a family meeting when Rebecca would introduce this need and ask for changes from every single one of them.

But, Rebecca was *terrified.*

Terrified that training and supervising her family on household tasks would be a lot of work on her end (yes, I see the irony). Terrified of the hard, uncomfortable conversations. And terrified more than anything of her family refusing to change. Despite us having several talks about her having *the talk* with her family, Rebecca kept putting it off. And we both knew the real reason why: her fears were winning.

How Past Failures Feed Current Fears

Many women carry a "What's the point?" attitude when it comes to requiring their family members to do more at home. In the past, they've likely tried to create some shifts to the household systems—that is, everyone doing more of their part—only to find themselves dejected and depleted by both the endless micro-managing and the lackluster results.

I've helped many, many women create systematic shifts in their homes, and I've heard their fears:

What if . . .

- My family hates me.
- They think I don't see how they *do* try, and everything coming from me feels negative and critical.
- These shifts lead to a lot of tension, resentment, and anger in the family.
- Their standards don't match my own.
- I have to be a drill sergeant and boss everyone around all of the time.
- It creates more work for me.

- I run out of energy and stop following through.
- Nothing changes.

That last one is most often the biggest underlying fear of all. And it's why I see women delay introducing these changes to their families—whether that family includes a roommate, a spouse, or children. In many ways, they're right to put off these household shifts. After all, many of their fears have been realized in the past and nothing really changed in the end. It was a lot of work for nothing.

But, there's a few common reasons why nothing changed in the past. First, the past attempts at systematic household changes were done like anything else related to invisible labor—women took on the full work themselves. Other family members did not truly understand nor value the deeper, underlying reasons for the desired changes. Also, the real purpose for these shifts ("Mom can't do it all anymore, please help!") got misplaced with lists of chores and multi-stepped, intense systems with women *still* being in charge of distributing, overseeing, and often stepping in to complete the assigned tasks. Striving for household shifts entailed women acting as both the head boss *and* the head servant, at the same time.

Shifting your home's systems *will* absolutely require work, with you holding the lion's share of it—at first. But these shifts should be taken on in different ways than you've done before, from leading with love and making decisions collaboratively, to ensuring the whole end goal of this pursuit is you *not* having to be the home's drill sergeant *or* fall guy forever and ever, amen.

That all starts with shifting the goal post: you have to get real about what you *actually* need to see change the most—and it's not just the toilet getting scrubbed without you having to remind a kid to do it. (Although, that's definitely part of it.)

In our last conversation before the talk, I reminded Rebecca, "The first time we worked through why systematic shifts in your home are necessary, I asked you what the ultimate goals were for you: what really mattered in terms of the changes you need to see out of your family that transcend who does what. Do you remember how you responded?"

Rebecca pursed her lips and nodded her head, recalling her words, "Yes. I want them to be more aware and I want them to take more ownership."

Start Here: Awareness and Ownership

Even if it's your choice, when what you do all day every day is invisible to others, it will eventually make *you* feel invisible. This has been true for each one of my coaching clients, even those who willingly adopted traditional gender roles in the home. Some day and somehow, when women's invisible loads go too far for too long, *all* women find themselves confessing that they feel resentful of their lives.

> **Women don't only want their families to do more, they want to be more *seen* and to be less responsible for *everything*.**

The biggest shifts a family needs to make in their homes start much, much deeper than who is doing what. It's far more about *awareness* and *ownership* of who is doing what. Once things are fully *seen* they can be truly *owned*, and once they are owned they can be better *valued*, and once they're valued they can be more consistently *executed*.

When a woman sets out to make shifts in how the labor is divided at home, the point isn't even to divide everything equally, like, "One for me, one for you." It's more about equally valuing our time, something Eve Rodsky teaches a great deal about in her book, *Fair Play*.[2]

Shifts in the household that are strictly about dividing the chores evenly will only lead to burnt-out "momagers" and unsustainable changes. Of course, there needs to be a better distribution of chores, but starting there is a superficial fix that won't address foundational, more persistent problems. Instead, when we begin deeper, then the practical changes will be more sustainable.

This is where awareness and ownership come in. These deep principles act as both the path *and* the goal of better distributing essential labor in your home. When you begin to talk about what you need to be different, I recommend leading with these principles as the foundation to everything:

- Awareness needs to happen in two ways. First, more broadly as family members better acknowledge what is *truly* involved in running a household. Second, more in the moment with individuals noticing tasks that need to be done.
- Ownership will look like each person taking on *full* CPE (remember conception, planning, and execution from *Fair Play*?)[3] over tasks that fall under their responsibilities, whether chosen or assigned (ideally, collaboratively). They will do so as needed and when noticed, without someone else having to nudge or nag.

It is also super important to communicate your *why* to your household. Here are some reasons past clients have stated:

- Living as part of a community, however big or small, requires *everyone* to contribute.
- Mom is a person, too.

---

[2] Eve Rodsky, *Fair Play: A Game-Changing Solution for When You Have Too Much to Do (and More Life to Live)* (Penguin Random House, 2021).

[3] A reminder of these standards from *Fair Play* by Eve Rodsky. She teaches that the most important organization in the world—the home—should adopt practices successful business organizations follow. That includes full CPE (conception, planning, and execution) of individual tasks.

- The primary caretaker deserves her efforts to be both validated and shared.
- Each person deserves to have a life that isn't just about checking off to-dos.
- A more fair division of labor will lead to a happier household.
- Children will leave the house one day and be part of homes and potentially families of their own; parents are in the business of preparing them.
- *Everyone* would benefit from less nagging.

With these deeper targets at play, then comes the honest question: "How?"

It all begins with talking. Lots of talking.

Communication

Rebecca finally assigned a date and time for the talk with her family: that very afternoon. But, I could tell that the fears were poised to win. I spoke up, "Rebecca, I know you're scared, but I want you to remember that the talk you need to have with your family won't be the only one. In fact, this work will entail a series of conversations. The first one is just about opening the door and inviting everyone inside."

Communication is *the* key to creating lasting shifts in a household. As you move into this pursuit, it's far better to know that this will not be a one-and-done kind of chat. That expectation is likely what led to disappointment in the past: you told everyone to do better and expected it to just happen. They failed, and you gave up. Instead, now you must expect that there will be many, many talks—both formal and informal.

These conversations can be *What About Bob*[4]–style baby steps that gradually introduce needs, help your household see your own point of view, and what you deeply want for every member (awareness and ownership), then eventually have more practical

[4]This is a popular comedy film from 1991with Bill Murray and Richard Dreyfuss.

chats on who is doing what. Regular check-ins should follow to monitor how things are going for everyone. (I recommend weekly family meetings for a good while.)

With that said, there are other ways to ensure that these talks aren't met with, "Aw, man, not again!"

Collaboration

Building a new way of distributing the load is most successful when the whole family has some choice in how they contribute. Make decisions collaboratively! That doesn't mean *every* choice is done via groupthink. For example, you are more in charge than your kids. However, household members are more likely to buy in when they have actually been part of the decision-making process.

I find it helps to begin with things that are clearly under each individual's purview: bedrooms, closets, toys, and other possessions, backpacks, laundry, lunches, and even practicing instruments. Start this work by ensuring these responsibilities are truly being owned by the individual who is most affected by them, with full CPE, as much as developmentally appropriate.

I also encourage you to be willing to compromise on the standard of execution. If you want to *actually* do less and have your family members take on more, you're going to have to let go of some things. Sure, kids don't often see dirt and dust the way our eyes do. You need to decide what really matters. Main shared areas matter more to me, so I have higher standards there. When it comes to my kids' rooms, possessions, and even how they fold their clothes, I'm more flexible about what done looks like. I'd recommend you do the same.

Shared spaces such as bathrooms, kitchens, family areas, play rooms, and so on, come next. You can both compromise on standards and decide together how managing them looks, from rotating assignments to concrete "This is now your zone for a while." Same goes with tasks like cooking or organizing. Who's to say your kids can't learn how to make dinner or clean out the family coat closet?

Whatever you choose, clarity of both frequency and what "done" looks like will be necessary for these systems to function.

I find that it works better for shared spaces to be divided into multiple tasks, and then different individuals can have full CPE ownership of assigned tasks rather than the whole room. This is true for us with the kitchen. While I oversee the whole room, my kids each have full ownership of certain chores that make the morning cleanup easier. Examples include emptying the dishwasher, packing and putting away leftovers, wiping the counters, and sweeping the floor.

The main point here: not everything has to be regimented and divided under individual CPE jurisdiction for you to be doing things right as a family. In truth, I'm betting it's the personal kinds of tasks that need to be prioritized the most (bedrooms, toys, clothes, etc.), with shared spaces coming later. Take it one to two responsibilities at a time, collaborate where possible, check in often, and then build onto the next tasks once the others are stable. And allllll along, remember you are teaching an old dog new tricks.

Reinforcement

I'm not saying you can train your family like a dog, but I'm not *not* saying that . . .

All the brain hacks we've used to help you train yourself to establish sustainable habits can reasonably and ethically be applied to involving your family in the home. Consider brain hacks such as the When-Then Pairing, practicing, lowering or raising the hurdle, and, most especially, rewards.

Reinforcement usually shows up via consequences. Since we want you to step away from embodying the angry momager stereotype, you can even collaborate on what the consequences will be when certain tasks are left unmet. Come to an agreement in advance, make sure they are clear, and then challenge yourself to step back and let the consequences follow.

Behavior design requires results that reinforce the desired behavior. Alas, this is where some of the work will lay for you by matter-of-factly following through. However, consequences shouldn't all be negative; in fact, your main challenge is to **make positive reinforcement the most common consequence** for when your people follow through.

Increased awareness is one of the biggest shifts you're making as a family, and that awareness must include calling out the *good* you see. Get used to saying things like, "I noticed you walked away from your shoes at first, but then remembered to put them away—well done!" "Hey, you did a great job keeping your room clean this week." Don't be above giving a literal pat on the back. This spirit of noticing will spread, and you will be on the receiving end, too.

Few things have made me feel more seen lately than when my 12-year-old son calls out the typically unnoticed tasks I do for the family. This very morning, he gave me an actual hug to thank me for making French toast for breakfast. (I know, *sob!*) The other day, he told me, "Mom, the car looks so clean! Thanks for vacuuming it out." This is not because I have an angel as a son. It's because we as a family have *all* worked to be more aware of what running a household entails. While that includes me as a mom noticing and validating what everyone else is doing, they're doing it more for me, too.

The consequences of reinforcement can also show up as literal rewards, from more screen time to family bowling nights, pizza parties, movie outings, or whatever floats your fun boat. In fact, prioritizing fun is something I encourage doubling down on as these shifts begin. You'll want to counteract the tension and create some real camaraderie because, after all, you really are in this together.

Break the Household's Bad Habits

Households often fall into unintentional habits that set you up as the primary responder, fixer, or organizer. Try to notice these habits and instigate shifts so other family members can properly do their part with more awareness and ownership.

Here are some examples:

- Automatically picking up your kids' shoes, backpacks, jackets, and so on → leaving items where they are and requiring kids put their own things away before certain privileges, like screen time
- Being the only one your kids call/text with needs → including Dad on those messages so he can help, too
- Driving forgotten lunches, homework, clothing items to school → deciding together which items you're okay taking to school for which children (where age appropriate), and what the alternatives are, such as the child eating school lunch instead or doing an extra chore at home to balance out the time your delivery required
- Being exclusively in charge of adding all kid events (practices, lessons, games, parties, school events, etc.) to the family calendar → Carrying the expectation that if plans are made/requested/confirmed, that parent/child adds the event to the family calendar
- Attending all parent teacher conferences, school meetings, PTA fundraisers, classroom volunteer opportunities → Trading off attendance with partner, and/or assigning certain kids to certain parents to monitor and attend on behalf of that child/children for the school year

Self-Ownership

While one of the main goals of making shifts in your home's systems is increased ownership from each family member, the most important ownership lies internally with you: you must embody your position as the Changemaker of your home.

Things absolutely need to be different. Those you love likely have neglected *seeing* you and what you contribute too much, and for too long. You deserve to be on your family's list, just like they saturate your own.

And yet, you have to own for yourself that these are living, breathing humans, and therefore are complicated. It will be challenging for them to make these shifts.

Additionally, you must acknowledge that you (even unknowingly) also participated to some extent in building and perpetuating these same systems. The hardest truth about invisible labor? Sometimes, we as women *keep* it invisible.

Many women fall into the Martyr trap, doing everything while quietly feeling exhausted, unseen, and resentful. We don't start our families this way; it usually begins with good intentions:

- "I want to take care of my family."
- "I want things done well."
- "I don't mind helping."

But, over time it can turn into this:

- Doing tasks no one else notices.
- Feeling responsible for *everything*.
- Believing no one else can do it right.
- Quietly simmering with resentment.

Here's the painful part: when we keep doing everything, others never get the chance to *see* the work, value it, and learn to share it. So, the cycle continues. You carry more, they notice less, you feel more invisible, you carry even more.

Breaking the Martyr trap doesn't mean caring less, it means shifting your role from Martyr to Changemaker. From doing everything, to leading shared responsibilities; from silent resentment, to honest communication.

Being a Changemaker is less about being the drill sergeant or momager; it's more about being the coach. It's seeing the big picture, knowing the playbook, and directing the work in ways that may be hard, but ultimately for everyone's benefit. It's molding future leaders, it's encouraging those forgotten on the team, it's owning that this work transcends the fundamentals of who is doing what, to instead focus on how everyone can better contribute and value each other's contributions. While there is no *I* in "team," you are the coach, so start leading.

This requires that you actually *choose* these changes. And as part of that, you *choose* the process to get there. Because it won't be pretty. It will take work, and there will be disappointments and failures along the way.

What likely went wrong for you in the past is that your despair led to resentment. Perhaps unreasonable expectations perpetuated the cycle over and over again. You may have even been so disappointed from the failure that you decided to withdraw altogether. However, when you *really* choose to be the Changemaker of your home, the work will feel different because *you* are different. And you're also doing this in a different way.

If you need to be reminded of this choice on occasion, if you get tired and fall off your own wagon, if resentment and nagging creep back in, just know that's all part of the process, too. Perfection isn't required for progress, so stop letting the all-or-nothing cycle stop your household from changing.

There Is No One-Size-Fits-All Approach

Before I move on from this chapter, I do want to acknowledge that even this tried-and-true advice may not be realistic for your circumstances. If you're a single mom, if your partner isn't willing or able to contribute to home life, if you are charged with especially heavy caretaking duties due to special needs in your home, or if you are experiencing anything that falls outside of what is typical, I must validate that this section may have felt unrelatable at best, and triggering at worst.

I will not pretend that there is a one-size-fits-all approach to increase support around the invisible loads you struggle to carry at home. But I can tell you that there *is* more help out there for you, whether that's an online support group that knows how you feel, or a therapist who can assist as you navigate this especially challenging season, or even hired out help if you can afford it. And most importantly, I want you to know that you are the ultimate expert of your own life. You know best what may work for you and what may not.

I encourage you to lean in and, as with habits, make your own prescriptions, challenge yourself to believe that change can still happen, and do something to take even the smallest of steps toward the more supported, fulfilling life you do, in fact, deserve.

One Changemaker's Results

Rebecca took that leap and things gradually, but then drastically over time, improved both for her and her family. She had been so afraid, but in starting with one small step (a simple conversation), big shifts followed. Little by little, Rebecca picked up sewing as a new hobby, had the time to take herself to breakfast most Saturday mornings, and found she was able to rest more in her very own home (which was no longer such a novelty!).

Despite her worries that these shifts would pressure her family (and they did), Rebecca's relationships with her husband and kids were actually less strained overall. Communication was happening often with nearly weekly family meetings, and more fun was the norm, too. Their family culture was shifting for the better. Rebecca felt less worried about her son's upcoming high school graduation and launch into adulthood. She knew was doing right by her younger daughter, too, in more ways than one.

With these results, Rebecca felt more confident about her pursuit to share more of the home labor. Of course, there was still room for improvement, but Rebecca felt motivated to continue her efforts. When she stopped to consider it, she could see that in changing the way her family carried the invisible labor that was once solely hers, she was molding how things would be better for her children's future homes, as well.

Rebecca wasn't just a Changemaker, she was a Cycle Breaker.

Before we move on from Part Five (and end the book—*can you believe it?!*), we need to revisit our other favorite teacher, Jill, and wrap up her habit story.

JILL

To advance her progress even more, Jill recognized that she was taking on too much at home and in ways where it felt like she was working a second shift. She chose to ask her husband to make dinner a few nights a week and take on an additional chore or two, like vacuuming. She allocated some of her paycheck to grocery delivery and store-prepped lunches for her workdays to lighten her own morning load. Jill also gently let her daughter know that she needed more warning to babysit the grandson she was obsessed with. She wanted to ensure she was taking care of herself in order to properly care for him. These changes felt small, but they were adding up. Jill felt more certain, more in control, and more like herself than she had in years—and ready to take on the hard decisions and possibilities attached to her next act: retirement and beyond.

TAKEAWAYS: While women can't wait until invisible labor improves to start prioritizing themselves, better distributing home labor is part of the big picture to being a happy woman with supportive habits. The goal isn't even distribution of home tasks—it's more awareness and more ownership from all household members. To make this happen: communicate, collaborate, reinforce, shift household habits, and own your place as the Changemaker (not momager) of your home.

(continued)

(continued)

TAKE THOUGHT: What is your end goal for changing the distribution of labor in your home? What fears do you have about leading this effort, and how can you meet them? What is one way your household can start small to build awareness and ownership?

TAKE ACTION: Have the first conversation (of many!) with your family where you share about what invisible labor is, how it happens at home, and why you'd like things to shift.

NOTE: For more (printables, recommended books, complementary podcast episodes, etc.), remember to check out the free and included Sticky Habit resources, available online at https://stickyhabitsbook.com/resources:

Epilogue: You Can Change

I was bouncing a fussy newborn in my arms—one who seemed insatiable, but wouldn't nurse and wanted Mommy at all times. It was 3 p.m. and I still hadn't showered or changed out of my PJs. Every part of our home looked like a series of mini-explosions had been set off. The sink was packed with dirty dishes, the dishwasher clean but full. Laundry baskets of unfolded clothes scattered throughout the main room. The fridge was empty but littered with crumbs, the pantry cupboards similarly bare. Unpaid bills piled up on the kitchen counter, church and social events were neglected entirely, and I hadn't so much as gone for a light walk—my main form of sanity each day.

And I wasn't new to this! The fussy newborn? My fifth child.

My fourth and fifth kids were born a little under five years apart. At 36 years old, that geriatric pregnancy, delivery, and recovery made for the hardest long-term physical feat of my life. I'll spare you the litany of ailments, symptoms, and complications that came up—just know I could give them a chapter of their own. I'm more of a realist when it comes to anything pregnancy, birth, and childrearing. I had done this four times before, so I thought I knew what I was getting into. With this last pregnancy behind me, I expected to adjust fairly quickly to my postpartum life. Sure, the pregnancy was awful, but with the baby out of my belly and in my arms, I'd be fine! But I was wrong.

The gap between my final two children made all the newborn knowledge in my head go poof! I was Googling how often to nurse him. I took an online course on sleep training out of pure desperation. While I cognitively knew how much work nurturing a little body would entail, I forgot what it *felt* like in *my* body. I was the kind of fragile, exhausted, overwhelmed, and anxious you typically see in first-time moms. And to top it all off, I felt like I couldn't even enjoy this final baby as I had hoped. It was all so much work, and yet it didn't look like I was getting *anything* done. The part of me that is a productivity powerhouse scoffed at my lack of accomplishments. If I was struggling with the barest of tasks, how would there ever be time for *me* in any way, ever again?

The most demoralizing part of everything was how it felt like I was losing myself. It was so easy to once again feel like the Martyr of the home and to never prioritize myself. When I glimpsed myself in the mirror, I saw a past version of "Monica" who was lost to her responsibilities. Looking ahead to several more years of toil and self-sacrifice that rearing a baby to toddler entails, I worried it would be a while before I could feel like myself again. My old fears resurfaced, ones that told me, "See! You can't change."

Can I Change?

This is perhaps the biggest underlying fear I see women face: What if *nothing* changes? What they really worry about when they vocalize that fear is, "Can *I* change?" Or even, "Am I too *broken* to change?"

One of my first clients admitted to that final fear aloud. Because it was a group coaching call, I could see her statement resonate with many other women on my computer screen filled with their nodding heads and sympathetic faces.

I couldn't lie to her—much of her life was indeed broken, meaning it wasn't working, healthy, or what anyone would desire for themselves. But I also knew a truth, and it's one I could boldly share with her and every woman on the call, "You may feel broken, but you are not unusually or irrevocably broken."

Nobody's life is perfect. Everyone needs at least some things to change, from the menial to the momentous. After interviewing hundreds of people who have made great strides in reshaping their lives, I've found most will tell you three things about change:

- It takes time.
- It is incremental.
- There is no arrival. There will always be room to grow.

When I first began treatment for my eating disorders at 20 years old, things got a lot worse before they got better. As I clawed my way toward healing my brain, my old patterns reared up and tore back at me in return; they did *not* want to release me from their clenches. That first year was the hardest and while I made improvements, they seemed so insignificant compared to where I desperately wanted to be. They also came at such a high cost. It was a minute-by-minute effort, one in which I had to remain vigilant at all times. I found it all exhausting and demoralizing.

Right when I felt I had hit rock bottom (again!), I had a therapy appointment in which I anguished over my state. I asked my therapist, "When will I get better?"

He sagely responded, "Monica, this will likely be something you'll carry the rest of your life."

I'm sure there are people who would think this was a terrible thing for my therapist to say. How hopeless of him! But for me, hearing that I didn't have to heal myself overnight freed me to persist in a new way. In accepting that this would be a long road, I was able to *stay on it*. In understanding that change would be messy and hard, I was allowed to do so imperfectly. Each mistake didn't make *me* a mistake. I could be human and still be pursuing progress.

I can tell you that now, 20 years later, I do *not* carry those issues even close to the extent I did before. In fact, I honestly would describe myself as "healed," at least as healed as a woman who lives in the 21st century could be. Even writing that all feels miraculous to me, as just a few years in, the changes were so incremental I truly believed that I would, in fact, struggle forever.

This different sort of persistence—one based on the acceptance that change is possible, imperfect, and takes time—has been replicated time and time again in my life, from hardships within my marriage to parenting special needs children.

If there is one thing I want you to take away from this book, even more than the tools of gaining and revising your habits, it's this: ***You can change.***[1]

To be even bolder, you *will* change—it's simply a fact and a matter of time, messy effort, and a whole lot of support. What *is* will not always *be*.

Remember, as long as you are pointed in the right direction and trying, then you are doing it right.

How to Stay on the Path to Progress

Overnight success is a myth. The people who appear to have experienced it either put in years of small, incremental, curvy progress you can't see, or their fast success is both unhealthy and unsustainable.

Plants that grow too quickly rarely last. Their roots are not strong enough to maintain their growth, causing them to break down sooner or not produce as healthy of fruit. Those that grow slowly grow strongly, from root to stem. I know you wish the

[1] My husband all but begged me to have you to search for a clip from *Rocky IV* where Rocky says something similar, so here is that suggestion!

change you desire would come quickly—I'm not immune to that longing. But if you want to transform in ways that are both deep and sustainable, then you need to get comfy taking the long (and sometimes lonely) path to progress.

The biggest thing that pushes people off that path is the belief that they are moving too slowly, and are therefore failing. They stop trying to make changes. "Gifted" people are most often those putting in the work and time. We forget that too easily. I see this play out in my daughter who many would describe as "talented" or even a "savant" with her artwork. While she has always had a proclivity to drawing and is extremely good at it for her age, what people don't see is how she paints and draws for hours each day.

Another thing that makes people disqualify themselves is the faulty belief of "arrival":

- "When I finally have that skill, I'll feel happy."
- "When I achieve that promotion, I'll be satisfied."
- "When I receive those accolades, I'll feel more secure."

Those who have embraced the long road also know that there is no real "arrival." There is *always* room to grow, and no success will make you feel that you are complete and done reaching for more. Instead, it's time to embrace that **the transformation lies in the process, not the outcome**. It's along the way that we can find out who we truly are, gain fulfillment, change our beliefs, and discover the deep and lasting joy that is available to us on this indirect path to progress. Are you willing to walk this path with me?

I succeeded greatly while in the overachieving phases of my past with perfectionism. And yet I paid heavy prices for my enviable outcomes, from my health to my sense of self to unsustainable growth. I never found what I was looking for in my achievements. I obviously made very little progress while in the underachieving phase of my perfectionism, and similarly paid for it, too. My fear of mistakes robbed me of the incremental growth I could have experienced.

Conversely, I have grown exponentially the last decade in my pursuit to refuse either side of this spectrum. It has required a different sort of courage to embrace messy progress, to believe that change takes time, and to know that I'll never "arrive." But, this has enabled me to transform in dramatic ways over time. This is what I want for you. This is what I know is available to you.

Where Am I Now?

Transitioning to five children was one of the biggest life shifts I've faced. My little boy's birth challenged everything I had taught for years about habits, identity, and progress. Most of my habits fell to the wayside, my hobbies were completely gone, and my postpartum anxiety coupled with my part-time job and primary parent responsibilities stretched my time and my bandwidth to the point where Martyr Monica became my own version of Sharon.

I came to a crossroads, one where I had to make a choice. Was I going to revert back to my old patterns? Was I going to allow the standards of self-sacrifice and perfectionism to rob me of *living* my own life? Or, would I choose to move forward by re-embracing the path I had adopted 10 years prior of "progress over perfection" as I worked to, once again, reclaim my life?

I chose to practice what I had preached, starting with owning that this was simply a season of my life—one that *would* require some shifts and even sacrifices, but that wouldn't be permanent. I talked back to Martyr Monica, reminding her that I had nearly 10 years of evidence that massive bumps in the road don't mean I am doing things wrong. I reminded myself that progress starts small and builds slowly.

Even more deeply, I had to take a hard look at something I thought I had made progress in—where my identity came from. With most of my typical productivity being blown to outer space, I had to reckon with the fact that I was still basing my sense of self on what I could do in a single day. I held firmly to a piece of advice lovingly shared by a member of my online community, "Being present is being productive."

While it has taken me nearly three years since that final birth, I am proud to say that most of my habits are back in action. I will also be honest in telling you that I experienced a major burnout this fall, one that forced me to own that I need more time for *me*—moments when tasks can be replaced with things like sewing, reading a book in front of the fire, or puttering around my garden. I'm in the very messy middle of sorting through how to reclaim some of my time so that I can have a life that is made up of more than a never-ending, urgent to-do list. With a book launch coming, I am owning that I may need to take on fewer coaching clients, limit my kids' extracurricular activities, and perhaps even hire a house cleaner and give back some of our weeknight family dinner responsibilities to Brad.

However it looks though, I know I can sort through it, I will find my way, and progress will not only come, it is happening right here, right now. There's room to grow, but I'm well on my way. I'm doing it right.

You Are Doing It Right

As you journey on your own path to progress, don't let the mess dissuade your persistence. As long as you're pointed in the right direction, change is coming. In truth, it's already happening. You may not be able to see it just yet, but you are doing it right.

Start now by honoring the fact that you read this entire book—no small feat! Then, decide for yourself one area of your life you need more support in and what habit can help you get there. As you move through the Sticky Habit Method, do so courageously, compassionately, and with curiosity.

I know that with time and practice, you'll find that your habits stick better than ever. I anticipate the thrill that making progress will bring to you. I can't wait for you to reclaim your life and your happiness along the way.

Most importantly, I look forward to you experiencing the greatest transformation this process brings: being able to show up to *your* life feeling like *yourself*.

Glossary

Adding An option to intentionally build a habit by adding on the next habit from an ideal routine.

Baselines The smallest and simplest version of ideal habits.

Brain Hacking Forming habits is less of a character thing and more of a brain thing. Brain hacks are ways to train your brain to form sticky habits.

CPE From Eve Rodsky's book, *Fair Play.* Adopting business systems, home tasks should follow full conception, planning, and execution by the people over them.

The Deep Breath A quick, but dependable, way to lengthen the Response Gap between trigger and reaction—taking one long, deep breath.

Four-Day Sprint A intentional way to install a habit. For four days straight, focus on implementing your new habit.

GMGMs Good Men with Great Methods. Male professionals who teach about habit formation, time management, and productivity, but in ways largely absent of considering how women's lives are different. Also known as "bro self-help" or "bro habit methods."

Habiteers Habit types that reveal the pitfalls women often fall into while defining and forming habits: Martyr, Dropper, Overachiever, and Dangler.

The Implementation Cycle The life cycle to forming habits: plan, practice, do, and tweak.

Invisible Labor The literal and mental/emotional labor performed to keep homes, communities, and institutions running that is largely undervalued, unpaid or underpaid, and unseen.

Maximizing An option to intentionally build a habit by doing more, building toward the ideal.

The Three Ns A way to examine bad habit's patterns over time. notice, name, and next.

OG Baseline The original baseline you used while forming a new habit, one that is always available to you.

Practice A brain hack! Train your brain in advance to better remember the habit.

The Process Small wins build over time.

Progress Cycle A pattern that can be used for good. The way we behave affects the way we see ourselves, and the way we see ourselves shapes the way we behave.

Response Gap The space between trigger and reaction. Also known as the space between *when* and *then*.

Revolutionizer A woman who redefines habits and the habit formation process. She believes in and practices The Process. She learns from her failures. And she follows the Sticky Habit Method to form supportive habits that stick for the season she needs them in.

Sally Down the Street An archetypal woman referenced to illustrate concepts.

Shame Cycle A shame-based pattern that can be used for bad. The way we behave affects the way we see ourselves, and the way we see ourselves shapes the way we behave.

Sticky Habit Formula Steps to follow to create a habit plan, centered on habit stacking and timing. *WHEN* (existing habit) + *THEN* (new habit) + *AFTER* (positive reinforcement). Often referenced in a shortened way, WTA.

Sticky Habit Method A guide for busy women to form supportive habits that stick.

Sticky Habit Matrix A collection of four habit maxims that make a habit sticky, each with its own ring: supportive, small, simple, and specific.

Sticky Habits Habits that help you to be consistent but also consistently *you*.

Sweet Spot Where all the rings from the Sticky Habit Matrix meet to ensure a habit can last.

When-Then Pairing The first two steps of the Sticky Habit Formula.

Win-Win Formula An acronym to objectively help gather information about a failure, missteps, or even a win. WN = What went ***w***ell? what did ***n***ot? + WIN = ***w***hat's ***i***mportant ***n***ow?

WTA *WHEN* + *THEN* + *AFTER*. Steps from the Sticky Habit Formula that make up a habit plan.

Zoom Out A way to step back and take an objective look at what really is happening.

Afterword

To help you embrace this different way of thinking and doing, I want to revisit the real women's stories featured more prominently throughout this book as a touchstone for what kind of progress is waiting for you. A "Where Are They Now" update is included in the free online resources. Their *afters* won't be the typical *happily ever after* (aka, "everything is perfect!") you see in other self-help spaces. Instead, I will share these women's current "messy middles" at the time of writing this book, celebrating the growth they have gained while honoring what they are working toward now.

NOTE: For more (printables, recommended books, complementary podcast episodes, etc.), remember to check out our free and included online resources here https://stickyhabitsbook.com/resources:

If you'd like to learn more specifically from me, consider the following:

- Listen to my podcast, *About Progress*, wherever you get your podcasts. The included free online resources directs you to where you can find the top episodes I recommend listening to that pair nicely with this book.
- Visit my website for more free-to-affordable offerings from online trainings to workshops, and to sign up for waitlists for my one-on-one coaching and membership program: www.aboutprogress.com.
- Follow me on Instagram and YouTube at @aboutprogress.

Thank you for reading!

Acknowledgments

Publishing my first book taught me a great deal, one of the biggest lessons being that you can't accomplish a major life goal alone.

I first want to thank my husband, Brad, for his inexhaustible support of me and this pursuit. From willingly pouring over my manuscript to taking over all caretaking tasks for our kids during important phases of the process, I couldn't have done it without him. Brad, you are the kind of man I hope all men aspire to be. To my children, I want to say thank you for acting interested in "Mom's book," being patient with the process, and celebrating every milestone alongside me.

Gratitude is also due to my friends and family who cared about and supported this dream. I want to especially thank my parents—Gary and Camille—as well as my in-laws—Bob and Shelley—and each of my six siblings and their spouses.

Special thanks is owed to my advanced readers who spent a great deal of time reading through my manuscript, offering up edits, suggestions, and encouragement, all of which were sorely needed. This book was made all the better thanks to your insight: Ashley Busby, Aubrey Klein, Candace Little, Heather Oyler, and Jennifer Criego.

This book was made possible thanks to the leadership and shepherding of Sam Osman from Jossey-Bass. Thanks to the full team who carried the invisible work of publishing, including Christine O'Conner, Sophie Thompson, Riley Webster, Susan Geraghty, Trinity McFadden, and countless others from book design to marketing. It's a gamble to bet on a first-time author. Thank you all for taking that chance on me.

Finally, to the podcast listeners, coaching clients (a few who are heavily featured in this book), and members of my book launch committee: I am lucky to be inspired daily by your courage, benefit from your intellect, and get motivated by the changes you make. Thank you for sticking with me and my work for this long, for opening doors I couldn't, and cheering me on when I felt defeated. I hope you can see yourself reflected in this book.

About the Author

Monica Packer is a longtime podcaster and founder of *About Progress*, a top-rated show with millions of downloads. She guides women to find sustainable growth by adopting progress over perfection. She has served thousands of women online as a certified habits and identity coach.

Monica is a mom of five, former middle school teacher, sourdough obsessor, and beginning gardener. She lives in Salt Lake City with her husband, Brad, and their children. This is her first book.

Index

C

D

E

F

G